THE COUNSELOR EDUCATOR'S GUIDE

Jude T. Austin II, PhD, LPC, LMFT-A, NCC, CCMHC, has a PhD in counselor education and supervision, and he is a licensed professional counselor, licensed marriage and family therapy associate, nationally certified counselor, and certified clinical mental health counselor. He is currently an assistant professor in the Professional Counseling Program at the University of Mary Hardin Baylor and serves as the program's clinical coordinator. He is also in private practice in Temple, Texas, working with individuals, couples, and families. His research focuses on counselor education pedagogy, specifically finding ways to help counseling students develop therapeutic presence in session. He is also the coauthor of the books *Counselor Self-Care* and *Surviving and Thriving in Your Counseling Program.*

Julius A. Austin, PhD, LPC, NCC, has a PhD in counselor education and supervision, and he is a licensed professional counselor and nationally certified counselor. He is currently a clinical therapist and the coordinator for the Office of Substance Abuse and Recovery at Tulane University. In this role, he serves students struggling with substance abuse issues and works with other academic and local community resources to support students in recovery. He is also an adjunct professor at Southeastern Louisiana University and Southern University and A&M College. His research focuses on counselor development and training. He is also the coauthor of the books *Counselor Self-Care* and *Surviving and Thriving in Your Counseling Program.*

THE COUNSELOR EDUCATOR'S GUIDE

Practical In-Class
Strategies and Activities

Jude T. Austin II, PhD, LPC, LMFT-A, NCC, CCMHC
Julius A. Austin, PhD, LPC, NCC

SPRINGER PUBLISHING COMPANY

Copyright © 2021 Springer Publishing Company, LLC
All rights reserved.

Springer Publishing Company, LLC
11 West 42nd Street, New York, NY 10036
www.springerpub.com
connect.springerpub.com/

Acquisitions Editor: Rhonda Dearborn
Compositor: Amnet Systems

ISBN: 978-0-8261-6221-2
ebook ISBN: 978-0-8261-6222-9
DOI: 10.1891/9780826162229

20 21 22 23 / 5 4 3 2 1

The author and the publisher of this Work have made every effort to use sources
believed to be reliable to provide information that is accurate and compatible with
the standards generally accepted at the time of publication. The author and publisher
shall not be liable for any special, consequential, or exemplary damages resulting, in
whole or in part, from the readers' use of, or reliance on, the information contained
in this book. The publisher has no responsibility for the persistence or accuracy of
URLs for external or third-party Internet websites referred to in this publication and
does not guarantee that any content on such websites is, or will remain, accurate or
appropriate.

Library of Congress Cataloging-in-Publication Data

Names: Austin, Jude T., II, author. | Austin, Julius A., author.
Title: The counselor educator's guide : practical in-class strategies and
    activities / Jude T. Austin II, Julius A. Austin.
Description: New York, NY : Springer Publishing Company, LLC, [2021] |
    Includes bibliographical references and index.
Identifiers: LCCN 2019055645 (print) | LCCN 2019055646 (ebook) | ISBN
    9780826162212 (paperback) | ISBN 9780826162229 (ebook)
Subjects: MESH: Counseling—education | Teaching—education | Education,
    Medical, Graduate
Classification: LCC R727.4 (print) | LCC R727.4 (ebook) | NLM WM 18 |
    DDC 362.1/04256—dc23
LC record available at https://lccn.loc.gov/2019055645
LC ebook record available at https://lccn.loc.gov/2019055646

Contact us to receive discount rates on bulk purchases.
We can also customize our books to meet your needs.
For more information please contact: sales@springerpub.com

To our wives, Lindsay (Jude) and Megan (Julius):
Without your never-failing support and
encouragement, we would still be writing
this book.

CONTENTS

PREFACE

WHY WE WROTE THIS BOOK

Being a new counselor educator is hard. Chasing tenure while teaching prep or new classes every semester makes it harder. The courses are complex. Unfortunately, there is no class that sits you down and walks you through the counselor training curriculum, describing the courses, their objectives, important topics that must be covered, advice, considerations, assignments, and potential course schedules. We attempted to do all of that in this book. Our hope is that doctoral students and new counselor educators can use this book to better prepare for their courses.

Our target readers are current doctoral students who are about to graduate and suddenly realize that they are actually still a bit confused about what teaching a graduate counseling course entails. If our readers are like we were as doctoral students, they are concerned with just how little time is spent in counselor education and supervision doctoral programs discussing how to prepare and conduct a graduate counseling course from start to finish. Our readers may have also spent time wondering why counselor educators never taught the doctoral-level Teaching Practicum course. Essentially, you may feel unprepared to take over the role of instructor.

In addition to the doctoral student reader, this book may have also attracted new, nontenured faculty members thinking, "If they would only let me teach [Insert Favorite Course], I would [Insert Naive Notion]." By now you know you may be teaching one familiar course and three or four new courses that require preparation. We teach the courses that need to be taught. These courses often vary from semester to semester. We have been counselor education faculty members for 4 years, and a great majority of that time was spent teaching new courses—courses we did not teach before. We understand that this is part of the nontenured experience, but it is frustrating.

This book was inspired by our experience as unprepared doctoral students and frustrated new faculty members. While resources are given regarding course syllabi and capstone assignments, limited resources exist regarding strategies for preparing a new course and conducting day-to-day lectures. While it takes years to become an outstanding counselor educator, this book may help new faculty members feel better prepared to enter the classroom when they get assigned a new course. It is a book we wished we had while obtaining our doctoral degrees and entering into our first professorial positions.

HOW TO USE THIS BOOK

This book can be used as a primary or secondary textbook in a doctoral-level Teaching Practicum course in Counselor Education and Supervision programs. This book can also be used as a pocket handbook for new faculty members who want to better understand how all of the courses in the curriculum influence each other. If you are a new faculty member using this book, we suggest doing so after you have lost the battle in the faculty meeting for the courses you would have been great teaching. Sit down with your borrowed syllabi and this book. Let the suggestions in this book influence the development of your courses.

WHAT'S IN THIS BOOK?

Each chapter focuses on a course taught in Council for Accreditation of Counseling and Related Educational Programs (CACREP)-accredited programs. Some similar courses were combined into one chapter, such as Diagnosis, Assessment, Treatment Planning. We also combined extra tracks such as the Marriage, Family, and Child Counseling program and school counseling. The following is a list of the chapters and a brief description of their content.

CHAPTER 1: TEACHING COUNSELING STUDENTS TODAY

In essence, this chapter introduces the reader to concepts that are discussed in further detail throughout the book. We start with a discussion of the current literature related to teaching counseling students today. We then explain the concept of andragogy and how it relates to teaching counseling students today. We then discuss CACREP accreditation and what this means for teaching. Additional topics to be discussed in this chapter are syllabi development, course objectives, evaluation of student learning and progress, classroom management, use of technology, advising, and ways educators evaluate themselves and students day-to-day.

CHAPTER 2: ORIENTATION TO PROFESSIONAL COUNSELING COURSES

This chapter covers information and activities for professional counseling orientation courses. This type of course is typically offered at the beginning of most students' degree plan. It introduces students to the field and their career options should they choose to continue pursuing their degree. Students will be challenged to ask the question "Do I want this career path?" or "Am I cut out for this profession?" Helping students develop a secure attachment to their faculty and a healthy relationship with the counseling profession is critical in this course. Activities discussed in this chapter may relate to professional roles and functions, counselor self-care, advocacy, and credentialing, certification, and licensure. This chapter's discussions and activities attend to the CACREP standards in section 2.F.1.a-m.

CHAPTER 3: ETHICS COURSES

In this chapter, we examine courses that cover ethical, legal, and professional issues in counseling practice. In courses like this, students learn to utilize ethical decision-making based upon the standards of the American Counseling Association, their desired specialty area in counseling (school, marriage, couple, and family, etc.), and laws governing professional counselors. Activities discussed in this chapter relate to maintaining ethical behavior when fulfilling professional roles and functions. Other topics in the course for which activities and teaching strategies are discussed include distance counseling, referring a client, counselors' values, and advocacy. This chapter's discussions and activities attend to the CACREP standards in section 2.F.1.a-m.

CHAPTER 4: COUNSELING THEORIES COURSES

This chapter discusses the counseling theories courses. This course provides the student with a number of counseling approaches that can be applied to the therapeutic process. It familiarizes the student with the approach and practice of each of the theories presented. In this chapter, we provide a more in-depth introduction to the course purposes and objectives. We also include a review of the current literature and research related to counseling theories, including helpful online evaluations for students struggling to ascribe to a theoretical orientation. Activities in this chapter are geared toward helping educators facilitate a process where students can gain the competence to select the form of counseling approach that will be most effective and appropriate to assist clients, families, and groups toward the completion of identified treatment goals. This chapter's discussions and activities attend to the CACREP standards in sections 2.F.5.a and f and 5.C.a and b.

CHAPTER 5: DIVERSITY COURSES

Diversity courses are critical to a counselor's development. These courses build on the skills developed in other courses and prepare students to work with clients, couples, and families and in school systems on topics such as culture conflict and personal identity, gender and racial issues, sex and sexuality, lifestyle concerns, coping versus personal empowerment, and effective intervention models when working with ethnic and linguistic minorities, including building effective parent involvement programs. This chapter's discussions and activities focus on helping counselor educators teach the aforementioned topics to their students. This chapter's discussions and activities attend to the CACREP standards in sections 2.F.2.a-h.

CHAPTER 6: LIFE-SPAN DEVELOPMENT COURSES

These courses cover a great amount of content regarding an individual's development from conception to death. Human development courses help students view their clients from a developmental perspective with the understanding that development does not take place in isolation; rather human development is deeply embedded within and inseparable from the context of family, social network, and culture. This course is also designed to help counselors recognize the importance of individual and systemic influences on human growth and development. Some of the many topics for which this chapter's discussions and activities focus include theories of individual and family development across the life span, normal and abnormal personality development, addictions and substance abuse, and biological, neurological, and physiological factors that affect human development, among others. This chapter's discussions and activities attend to the CACREP standards in sections 2.F.3.a-i.

CHAPTER 7: COUNSELING TECHNIQUES COURSES

Counseling techniques courses provide foundational education in core counseling skills. Mastery of these skills throughout these courses ensures that counselors have the necessary tools to work effectively with clients as they move on to practicum and internship. Some of the topics this chapter's discussions and activities address are developing therapeutic presence; therapeutic listening; reflecting empathy to client, couple, and family concerns' case conceptualization; and crisis management. This chapter's discussions and activities attend to the CACREP standards in sections 2.F.5.a-n.

CHAPTER 8: CAREER DEVELOPMENT COURSES

This chapter focuses on career counseling courses. In this course, students learn how career development theory can be applied to the practice of career counseling. Students also learn how trait and factor theories provide a way to help individuals make career decisions based on assessment of interests, abilities, achievements, personalities, and values. This course also discusses the structure of the job market and information about specific occupations, including job duties, education, salary, and employment outlook. This chapter focuses its discussion and activities around these topics, as well as topics such as career development across the life span, the effects of racial and sex discrimination on individuals, labor market discrimination, affirmative action, and conducting a career counseling session. This chapter's discussions and activities attend to the CACREP standards in sections 2.F.4.a-j.

CHAPTER 9: GROUP COUNSELING COURSES

This chapter covers group counseling courses. These courses focus on effective group leadership skills and the dynamics associated with group process and development. The discussion and activities in this chapter address topics such as the theoretical foundations of group counseling, group counseling dynamics, group counseling techniques, group formation, screening, and ethically and culturally relevant group practice. This chapter's discussions and activities attend to the CACREP standards in sections 2.F.6.a-h.

CHAPTER 10: RESEARCH COURSES

This chapter focuses on another course that is the source of some students' anxiety. In fact, some prospective students choose not to apply to counseling programs and graduate schools because of research courses. This is an introductory-level graduate course that is designed to provide students with knowledge of the terminology, symbols, and methods employed in research. Further, this course focuses on the development of a fundamental level of research design necessary for interpreting and completing basic small-scale research and evaluation projects. The discussion and activities in this chapter cover topics such as research and the counseling profession, needs assessments, evaluating counseling interventions, statistical methods, use of data in counseling, and ethical and culturally relevant strategies for conducting research. This chapter's discussions and activities attend to the CACREP standards in sections 2.F.8.a-j.

CHAPTER 11: DIAGNOSIS, ASSESSMENT, AND TREATMENT PLANNING COURSES

These courses address diagnosis and treatment planning from a variety of perspectives: biologic, developmental, cultural, and interpersonal. This chapter provides students with a broad theoretical base for understanding psychopathology, not only from an individual, descriptive, symptoms perspective as presented in the *Diagnostic and Statistical Manual of Mental Disorders* (5th ed.; *DSM-5*; American Psychiatric Association, 2013), but also from a contextual systemic perspective, including developmental hallmarks, familial patterns, and sociocultural contributors. The discussion and activities in this chapter focus on the diagnostic process and nomenclature, treatment, referral, prevention of mental and emotional disorders, biopsychosocial case conceptualization, and appropriate counseling treatment plans. This chapter's discussions and activities attend to the CACREP standards in sections 5.C.2.d. and 5.F.2.d.

CHAPTER 12: PRACTICUM AND INTERNSHIP COURSES

Practicum and internship courses give students an opportunity to earn clinical experience at a local mental health site. These courses are designed to meet the CACREP accreditation standards and are based on seminar-style class discussion, the presentation and discussion of cases, clinical group supervision principles, and didactic instruction. Typically, programs require students to complete a clinically supervised practicum of 100 clock hours and an internship of 300 clock hours, which is to be fulfilled in an academic semester. The practicum and internship provide an opportunity for students to perform, under clinical supervision, a variety of professional counseling activities that a regularly employed staff member in the setting would be expected to perform. This chapter focuses discussions and activities on topics such as managing relationships, self-care, advocating for self and clients, receiving supervision, and more. This chapter's discussions and activities attend to the CACREP standards in section 3.F-M.

CHAPTER 13: MARRIAGE, COUPLE, AND FAMILY COUNSELING COURSES

These courses focus on helping students gain the necessary knowledge, skills, and attitudes to work with couples and families. These courses introduce students to the theory, philosophy, and methods of systems work. This chapter focuses discussions and activities on topics such as systems theories, evidence-based interventions, contextualizing families, and cultural factors relevant to marriage. This chapter's discussions and activities attend to the CACREP standards in section 5.F.1-3.

CHAPTER 14: SCHOOL COUNSELING COURSES

These courses focus on the professional issues faced by school counselors and prepare students to work with children and adolescents in school environments. These courses emphasize the contemporary role of the school counselor as leader and advocate in delivering school counseling programs to all students. Emphasis is placed on acquiring the awareness, knowledge, and skills necessary to negotiate the cultural, educational, and contextual forces that impact the lives and academic achievement of students in a pluralistic society. This chapter focuses discussion and activities on these topics and others, including school culture, learning, classroom management, structured groups, counseling children and adolescents, and program development. This chapter's discussions and activities attend to the CACREP standards in section 5.G.1-3.

REFERENCE

American Psychiatric Association. (2013). *Diagnostic and statistical manual of mental disorders* (5th ed.). Arlington, VA: American Psychiatric Publishing.

ACKNOWLEDGMENTS

Writing a book is challenging. We could not have accomplished this task if not for the support of those around us:

- To our wives, who had babies 6 weeks apart from each other and a couple of months before this book's due date. We are in awe of your strength and patience.
- To our parents, who supported us in so many ways throughout this project's journey. Thank you for speaking words of encouragement, babysitting kids, making food, and doing all the things parents do.
- To our sister, who will be Dr. Jasmine Austin by the time this book is printed. Your work ethic inspires us.
- To our past professors, specifically Drs. Leonard, Chou, Eary, Howard, Ballard, Statz, and Benner. You all showed us how to teach and learn well. Anyone can teach, but few can teach well. Thank you all for providing such a firm foundation in our careers.

- To our mentors, the good brothers Drs. Vereen and Ford as well as Dr. Kellie Kirksey, whose support propels us. The pride in your eyes when we meet at conferences and in your voice when we check in means more to us than you all will ever know.
- To Jerry and Marianne Corey—thank you both for believing in us. Thank you both for showing us how to stand our ground and have the kinds of careers that we can be proud of. We value our time with you both hiking and talking about this book as doctoral students and walking through cities while talking about life and careers. Not only are you both influential figures in our field; you both are caring and loving to us and our families. We will remain forever grateful.
- We want to acknowledge Mehak Massand and Rhonda Dearborn from Springer Publishing Company, who remained patient and understanding with us throughout every bump in the road of this project. This book would not be possible without your support.

1 TEACHING COUNSELING STUDENTS TODAY

INTRODUCTION

Are doctoral students prepared to fulfill the multifaceted role of counselor educator upon graduation? According to Elliott et al. (2019) and our own personal experiences, the answer is no, they are not fully prepared for the role of counselor educator. Elliott et al.'s (2019) study explored intentional pedagogical training in counselor education doctoral programs. The doctoral student participants' experiences mimics our experiences in that they shared feelings of fear and self-doubt, incongruence within the teaching role, and various levels of unpreparedness. No doctoral program can fully prepare new counselor educators for the ever-evolving roles and responsibilities of this profession. Hopefully, this chapter and the following ones can fill in the gaps.

Some counselor education doctoral programs prioritize training either effective educators or researchers. The focus usually aligns with the emphases of the university that supports those doctoral programs. It is known that current faculty promotion and tenure criteria strongly emphasize teaching over scholarship (Baltrinic, Jencius, & McGlothlin, 2016; Barrio Minton, Wachter Morris, & Yaites, 2014; Orr, Hall, & Hulse-Killacky, 2008). This shift is also reflected in the 2016 Council for Accreditation of Counseling and Related Educational Programs (CACREP) standards, where there is more importance placed on training doctoral students in instructional theory and pedagogy (CACREP, 2001, 2009). In fact, the 2016 CACREP standards plainly state that counselor education doctoral students must develop a professional identity related to teaching practices and responsibilities (CACREP, 2015a, Section 6.B.3). The caveat to this emphasis is that the CACREP standards are designed for programmatic flexibility. Training graduates who are highly effective teachers is not standardized across counselor education programs. Therefore, there is no way of knowing how effectively doctoral programs are prioritizing this component of their students' development (Malott, Hall, Sheely-Moore, Krell, Cardaciotto, 2014).

Despite which facet of education, research, or teaching a program prioritized, we have imagined that if you picked up this book, you are passionate about training counselors. You want to be effective but feel overwhelmed at times by the demands and responsibilities of a counselor educator. You should feel pressure; after all, the state of the counseling field and the mental health of generations rest upon your students' decisions in critical moments in session and their ability to build strong therapeutic relationships. When it sank in, when the gravity of our responsibility as counselor educators washed over us, it gave us pause. Everything we do and say in this role has ripple effects in the communities our students serve.

This book may be picked up at various stages of a counselor educator's career. Readers may be doctoral students in their first doctoral-level teaching course. They may have just graduated from a doctoral program in counselor education and supervision or a related field, bagged the first faculty position, and received the teaching assignments for the first semester. Or maybe readers are veteran professors with tenure, great teaching evaluations, and a bookshelf of awards and books, but who may occasionally feel off their game. However readers found their way to this book and this chapter, our hope is that by the end they gain a more enriched understanding of the contexts in which they are training students and the world they are preparing students to serve.

OVERVIEW OF INSTITUTIONS OF HIGHER EDUCATION

Universities are like Russian dolls. There is a community that engulfs a university (e.g., Arsenal University). Within Arsenal University there are multiple colleges (e.g., College of Education), which engulf programs (e.g., Counseling Program), which further engulf individual faculty members (e.g., Dr. Thierry Henry), who support students (e.g., Ian Wright). They are all nestled within one another and affect each other immensely. Our experience as counselor educators, and perhaps yours too, is that big decisions about the university are like a fog that slowly seeps into our offices. We find ourselves asking"When did we start doing it that way?" quite often.

Counselor educators may have accepted a position under the pretense that they have to publish only 8 to 12 articles in 5 years to keep their jobs. Then during the second semester, those counselor educators hear that they now need 12 to 15 published articles in top-tier journals. Then, a couple more months pass, and that number jumps to 15 to 20. And they risk losing their jobs unless awarded a grant. The counselor educators may then have to move themselves and their families to their next job. Sometimes counselor education can be a transient field. The system is not perfect. Training highly effective clinicians is not always the priority of the program or the university.

Decisions such as how much counselor educators publish and where they publish are influenced by stakeholders who have a tremendous influence over the characteristics of a university. There are a great number of universities in the United States, and it is hard to classify these institutions. However, in 1973 the Carnegie Classification of Institutions of Higher

Education provided ways to differentiate between institutions (Altbach, 2015). Briefly, Altbach (2015) explained that the Carnegie Classification tracks data such as the type and number of degrees awarded, faculty numbers, enrollment numbers, funds generated from intellectual property such as research or book publications, the amount of research projects conducted, and the level of internationalization. According to Okech and Rubel (2018), there are different types of institutions within the Carnegie Classification: Research Intensive and Others, Teaching Intensive and Others, and Traditional Online and Hybrid.

COUNSELOR EDUCATION

As counselor educators, we belong to a unique profession that closely relates to the evolution of the counseling profession. We, like clinicians, are supported by professional organizations, but ours are focused on training counselors: the Association for Counselor Education and Supervision (ACES) and the CACREP. The enduring advocacy by the ACES on behalf of counselor educators and supervisors has led to the development of standards for counselor preparation (ACES, 1979, 2014) and counseling programs (CACREP, 2015b). The heart of the ACES lies in the advancement of the counseling profession through counselor education and supervision (ACES, n.d.). Since its inception, the CACREP aimed to "provide leadership and to promote excellence in professional preparation through the accreditation of counseling and related educational programs" (CACREP, 2020).

Today, the CACREP standards shape the counselor education curriculum, which means that the CACREP has a significant influence over who we are as counselors and counselor educators. Counselor training programs are given a certain amount of freedom to meet the CACREP standards given the needs of the communities they serve, the culture of their institution, the cultural diversity of their program, and other factors.

The role of a counselor educator stretches well beyond the responsibilities of instruction. Counselor educators wear many hats while maintaining their role and responsibilities. They are asked to advise, mentor, gatekeep, administrate, serve both the professional and local communities, supervise, teach, and be part of many other activities. The position comes with a variety of nebulous relationships and stressors that doctoral students and new faculty members may feel unprepared to manage (Magnuson, 2002).

If we were new faculty members again, we would have asked to see the program's previous *CACREP Self-Study Report*. This report is a comprehensive overview of the counseling program. It includes narrative responses and supporting documentation that show how the program is meeting the CACREP standards. We would have read through the self-study and the current program handbook. We would have created a list of questions about the program and met with our department chair to talk through the program. Doing these things would have given us a better understanding of how the program operates and how we can best serve it.

Teaching Is Hard

Teaching counselors is hard because of its layered complexity. One minute counselor educators are using counseling skills in class, then supervising, then writing and conducting research, then presenting at a conference, then serving the community (maybe they have a small private practice), and then handling student concerns; or a clinical site is violating their supervision contract; or the CACREP report is due; or a supervisee needs to speak to a detective about his or her client. Each day is different, and managing this complexity comes with experience.

Perhaps the existence of transferable skills, or lack of it, between counseling and counselor educating is also hard. Counselor training, and to some extent counselor education training too, did not prepare me to impart vast amounts of information while attending to different student cultures and learning styles, assessing students' clinical skills and other work, and providing personalized feedback. If readers are like us at the beginning of their careers, they may have felt like an impostor. Like us, readers may be millennials, the youngest faculty members in their program and among the youngest in the university. This may cause readers to think, "I hope they don't figure out I am only one class day ahead of them in the reading."

We have found, like in our counseling work, we are most successful when we bring all of who we are into the room, build a strong therapeutic relationship, and relate the coursework to the lives of our students. Palmer (2017) reminds us that "bad teachers distance themselves from the subjects they are teaching—and in the process, from their students. Good teachers join self and subject and students in the fabric of life" (p. 11). Training counselors is hard because we are working with adults who have trauma, triggers, flaws, and strengths.

Common Theories of Teaching and Learning

In counseling, our theoretical orientation guides our work. This is true for the educational theory we choose to be the undercurrent of our teaching. In our experience, choosing a teaching theory that aligns with our counseling approach helped us feel more congruent in the classroom. Choosing a teaching theory also mimics the process of choosing a counseling theory; it takes time and patience. There are many theories of teaching and learning, and they are constantly evolving. We do not cover all of them, but only the seminal works within the extant literature.

Constructivism

A major principle of this theory is that the learner is an information constructor. The learning process is active and built upon the experiences of the student (McAuliffe & Eriksen, 2011; Vijaya Kumari, 2014). Students construct their own meaning from the lecture or classroom activities based upon their subjective experiences (Whitman & Beeson, 2018). There is no universal truth in this perspective. Your role is to help students expand their understanding of reality and construct their own truth. You facilitate an environment where students can use their own skills to solve life's problems. Constructivist educators use dialogue to spark active learning where students grapple with topics from within a social context (Whitman & Beeson, 2018). Counseling theories are not just words on a PowerPoint presentation for students to memorize to pass their exam. Students experience these theories, filter them through their life experiences, and reflect on what it means for them to understand a concept culturally, spiritually, or relationally. The constructivist perspective aligns with humanistic approaches to counseling. McAuliffe and Eriksen (2011) offer guidance to counselor educators wanting to teach from this perspective. Having known and taught alongside Garrett McAuliffe for a couple of years, I (Jude) saw how he encouraged his students' autonomy and engagement by beginning lectures asking students what they needed, educationally, in order to feel prepared to do their best work. I was struck by the relationship he was able to cultivate between students and the topics they discussed in class.

Critical Pedagogy

You may recognize characteristics from this theory from its inspiration: critical theory. According to Freire (2018), educators practicing critical pedagogy focus on power, oppression, injustice, and society in regard to economic, cultural, and political inequality. According to Aliakbari and Faraji (2011), "students should act in a way that enables them to transform their societies which is best achieved through emancipatory education" (p. 77). In our understanding, emancipatory education is an environment where students can question their instructor and the information presented in class. Freire (2018) explained that traditionally, teachings have a monolithic approach to education—teachers are the experts, and students unquestionably comply. The formula in traditional views of education is (a) students receive the teacher's knowledge, (b) memorize, and (c) repeat (Aliakbari & Faraji, 2011). Critical pedagogy places students in a more active role, where they take in knowledge and then apply it to societal issues such as oppression and racism with the goal to improve society (Freire, 2018). Students have a right to question and be heard (Nixon-Ponder, 1995). There is a sense of equality in the classroom environment, and it is student centered and involves critical thinking and discussions. At the end of the semester, students might say that a course taught from this perspective raises their consciousness and makes them more critical about the world. This theory might align with the feminist approach to counseling.

Transformative Learning

This theory was created by Mezirow in 1978 and suggests that we learn through the process of changing our frame of reference. Mezirow (2018) explained that individuals create their own frame of reference for the world based on their values, feelings, thoughts, assumptions, and life experiences. Over time, these properties shape our perspectives. They are influenced by culture, politics, and education (Mezirow, 2018). These influences are like codes in our minds and make up our point of view. Transformational learning emphasizes critical reflection of this point of view. The code gets updated as we confront the world around us through the topics discussed in class. The challenge for educators using this approach is creating an environment where students feel safe to reflect critically on their assumptions and stereotypes. Mezirow (2018) suggested that educators navigate this challenge by encouraging autonomous and critical thinking and empathic expression of thoughts and feelings. Remaining open to students' perspectives, regardless of our agreement or disagreement, can facilitate this classroom environment.

The Students

Graduate students learn best when treated like adults. Meaning, counselor educators must respect their time and the sacrifices they make to come to class and complete homework assignments. It is generally assumed that for adult learners, (a) self-concept becomes more self-directed because of maturity, (b) experience is an invaluable resource that informs learning and accommodates new information, (c) readiness to learn is based on performing social tasks more effectively, and (d) orientation to learning is based on present applications instead of future applications (Knowles, 1970). We believe these assumptions to be true for millennial learners too, who make up most graduate counseling courses today.

If readers are like us, they may have found themselves sitting awkwardly in a faculty meeting, the only millennials, discussing ways to better teach millennials. We have heard things like "This generation is so entitled." Are millennials the needy, entitled, selfish brats some older tenured faculty members believe us to be? The answer is "maybe," and so is everyone else. In a 2010 study, Stewart and Bernhardt compared millennial students with pre-1987 students. They found that millennial college students experience lower feelings of health and fulfillment, as well as less impulse control (Stewart & Bernhardt, 2010). They also found that millennial students scored higher on narcissism scales when compared to nonmillennials (Stewart & Bernhardt, 2010). However, their findings saw an increase in these factors across different student demographics, which led them to suggest that universities may just be admitting greater numbers of less healthy, more impulsive and entitled students in general, regardless of age (Stewart & Bernhardt, 2010). Gregg (2017) discussed millennial students from a developmental perspective. He suggests that emerging adulthood is a time for self-focus and making independent decisions, sometimes for the first time. From a distance, this learning process can seem like narcissism and impulsivity. We think sometimes professors forget that discernment is a learned trait, and not given to us at birth. And yes, we can admit that we and other members of our generation may have experienced a delayed entry into adult levels of responsibility, which causes us to need more attention at times. However, to blanket a whole graduate classroom with generation characteristics is dangerous.

The danger rests in not acknowledging the full spectrum of diversity within each counseling classroom today. Today's graduate counseling classrooms are more diverse than ever before. For example, some tenured faculty grew up when everyone in their house, on their street, in their neighborhood and city liked similar music. Today, siblings grow up in the same room and have a completely different cultural identity. They may share the same ethnic makeup, but one sibling loves mainstream pop music, while the other may have heard and fallen in love with an obscure comedy acoustic folk duet from New Zealand. One sibling may love golf and the other cosplay.

The access to information, self-defining experiences, and self-exploration activities are endless today, and our students take advantage of them well before they enter our classrooms. By graduate school, a student may have lived 10 virtual lifetimes, raised digital children, studied black holes, and have had access to answer every single question he or she may have had via his or her computer or cell phone. The challenge is not only respecting the diversity but addressing it in a way that supports all students' learning.

Today's students also face an increasing amount of pressure and concerns from the outside world than previous generations. Consider the cost of a graduate degree in counseling today; some programs range from $300 a credit hour to $900 a credit hour. Financial burdens can add more significance to their grade on a paper. A lower grade can threaten the sustainability of a small young family. The cost is far more than finical. Students pay in time—time away from their children, partners, parents, and other loved ones. Most nontraditional students live in dual income homes where the student and the partner work tirelessly to run their family while meeting the demands of a sometimes-empathetic course instructor. We have seen students who gave birth a week ago and are back for the next class. I (Jude) have had a student have a minor heart attack, the third one, and missed only two classes. We have seen students who are school teachers who also drive for Uber at the end of their school day and before our class starts. There are also students who struggle to participate in class because they are the primary caregiver for their child with special needs and aging parents. The sacrifices students make to pay this cost, in our opinion, give them the right to expect a certain level of training. These students need empathy, not sympathy. Empathy can support the energy they need to thrive in graduate school.

In addition to financial burdens, some students, especially those belonging to marginalized populations, face an increased threat to their lives and emotional well-being. Today's students come to class after a long day of facing microaggressions, exhaustive code switching, racism, sexism, gaslighting, and a host of other spirit-pounding interactions. Our class topics can be triggering depending upon students' lived experiences. Why would they not be exhausted by the time they make it to class? Why would they not be triggered by a discussion on privilege? We all know that students getting triggered is not a new phenomenon in counseling classrooms, but today's students are more aware of current issues; some can be more connected to these issues, which means that counselor educators have to stay abreast of current issues as well. Consider the current political climate. For readers who, like us, taught a class on the day after the 2016 presidential election, you know how much of an impact current issues have on students' development. Most of my classes postelection turned into a partisan group process where students from all political and religious affiliations shared their hearts. Again, after the "Kavanaugh hearing," we spent time in our practicum and internship classes discussing how the hearings influenced our students and their clients. It is more than technology and the Internet that influence today's students. They seem to be more connected to personal, community, and global issues. To connect with these students, we as counselor educators need to teach with this in mind.

What Do We Know About Counselor Development?

We know that counselor development is a gradual process where counselors move from relying on external authority to internal authority over a long period of time (Skovholt & Ronnestad, 1992). We also know that while training in graduate school has a great impact on counselor development, continued training after graduation and throughout a counselor's career may have an even greater impact (Skovholt & Ronnestad, 1992). You may already recognize the names Skovholt and Ronnestad from your readings about counselor development. They completed a seminal research project in 1992 identifying a stage model of counselor development. They also included themes related to counselor development.

In that study, Skovholt and Ronnestad (1992) identified eight stages of counselor development over the course of a long career. Those stages include (a) conventional—untrained professional using what one naturally knows, (b) transition to professional training—first-year graduate students who are working to assimilate a vast amount of information and apply it to practice, (c) imitation of experts—middle graduate school years where students maintain a meta-level openness but are uncertain while developing a mastery of the basics, (d) conditional autonomy—internship students who are functioning as professionals with variable confidence, (e) exploration—new graduates who are anxiously modifying externally imposed professional styles, (f) integration—2- to 5-year postgraduates who are developing authenticity, (g) individuation—characterized by a deepening of authenticity as wisdom and experience is accumulated, and (h) integrity—counselors are being themselves and preparing for retirement.

Skovholt and Ronnestad (1992) went on to discuss 20 themes related to counselor development. While they are all important, we choose the themes we believe to be particularly poignant to the larger discussion within this chapter. One theme within their research states, "Professional development is growth toward professional individuation" (Skovholt & Ronnestad, 1992, p. 507). Counseling students are constantly striving to integrate their personal and professional selves. Counselor educators must facilitate a classroom experience that sparks reflection upon these two parts of students as they grow. The next theme aligns with the previous statement: "As the professional matures, continuous professional reflection constitutes the central developmental process" (p. 509). They went on to discuss what is involved in professional reflection: intense personal and professional experiences, open and supportive work environment, and a reflective stance. Another notable theme suggests that "development is influenced by multiple sources that are experienced in both common and unique ways" (p. 511). This theme parallels what has been found to work in therapy.

According to Duncan, Miller, Wampold, and Hubble (2010), 40% of what works in therapy are client variables and extra-therapeutic events that are out of the therapist's control. Counseling graduate students are trained outside of the classroom as well as inside. As educators, we simply try not to allow their education to get in the way of their *education*. For example, as practicum students, we needed to process case after case, sharing insights and sometimes even dumping our lived experience. We felt our education getting in the way of our *education* when our instructor needed to discuss that day's journal article topics and book chapters that may not have been related to our caseload. This brings us to our next theme: "Clients are a continuous source of influence and serve as primary teachers" (Skovholt & Ronnestad, 1992, p. 512). The old counseling adage is correct: We get the clients/students we need. The universe has an interesting way of knowing which personal issues you have yet to resolve, and it pumps your caseloads and classrooms full of people who force you to confront those issues. Growth in some way is unavoidable when we use built-in teaching tools such as our students' clinical experiences. The last theme explains that "extensive experience with suffering produces heightened tolerance and acceptance of human variability" (Skovholt & Ronnestad, 1992, p. 514). This means: make your students suffer for their own good! Seriously, the researchers explained that mistakes and suffering in some form are an inherent part of life. As counselor educators, it may be beneficial to lean into this lived experience in class, making lectures and activities experiential and focused on acclimating students to the suffering they will hear in their work.

How Do They Learn?

There are as many ways to learn as there are people on Earth. The past 20 years have seen an increase in research regarding the way people learn. This research yielded general principles about learning that can guide our perspectives of counseling graduate students. According to Bransford, Brown, and Cocking (2000), our students are learning from birth and are more likely to learn what they think is relevant to their lives (Ambrose, Bridges, DiPietro, Lovett, & Norman, 2010). We must make students aware of the relevance of our lectures and classroom activities in their lives and to their work with clients. Students also learn by connecting previous knowledge to new knowledge (Wlodkowski & Ginsberg, 2017). Our students may come into our classrooms having had full and successful careers in other fields. We must help them connect that knowledge to their clinical work. For example, we have stay-at-home moms entering our program believing that they have nothing to offer until we highlight the years of practical listening and reflecting skills they have honed over the years with their children.

Additionally, students learn through interaction, as they co-construct knowledge (Barkley & Major, 2018). We believe learning through interaction parallels what works in therapy: genuine relational interaction. We have found that if at the end of the semester our students can say "We know who Dr. Austin is as a person," they also tend to retain course information. Students also learn when they are engaging in active learning opposed to passively listening to a professor lecture at them (Barkley & Major, 2018; Wilson & Korn, 2007). As in the previous principle, joining with students, closing the distance between their inexperience and our experience as faculty, engages them in the active learning process. Students' connection to the information often parallels their connections to the instructor.

Our students also learn when we design lectures that minimize cognitive load and lessen the demands on their working memory (Sweller, 2016). Our students' working memories are responsible for temporarily holding information available for processing. While it is essential to reasoning and decision-making, it has a limited capacity. Focus on the quality of the information and experiences with which we load students as opposed to the quantity. We believe every student would prefer a 30-minute lecture and two meaningful and engaging activities compared to 3 hours of a lecture with a 75-slide PowerPoint presentation. Lastly, according to Bjork (2017), our students tend to remember things longer when they have worked hard to learn them by overcoming desirable difficulties. This principle could be taken literally, causing you to make your classes harder to pass. However, we think of ways we can engage our students in a more challenging way during class. This may be done by creating inventive ways for students to process the course topics in small groups. Bjork (2017) suggested that counselor educators address this principle by raising their standards in the class and discussing this rise with students.

What Do They Need to Learn?

On one hand, students need to learn how to be the counselors we would feel comfortable allowing our loved ones to work with. On the other hand, we want them to pass the licensure exam. Sometimes, a counselor who can do both is difficult to develop. All counseling courses, especially courses in CACREP-accredited programs, focus on specific empirically based skills, knowledge, and attitudes needed to conduct effective counseling. To better answer this section's question, we need to know what makes counseling effective. By now it is no secret that for therapy to work, counselors must be proficient at developing a strong therapeutic relationship (Duncan et al., 2010).

The most accepted understanding of how to build a strong therapeutic relationship was developed and proven by Carl Rogers. He suggested that the therapeutic relationship was built upon the therapist's offered conditions of genuineness, unconditional positive regard, and empathy (Rogers, 1951). However, shortly before his death, Rogers said that by paying so much attention to these offered conditions, he ignored the most important element of effective therapy—being therapeutically present with clients (Austin & Austin, 2018; Baldwin, 2013). Other researchers confirmed the therapist's presence as an essential component of a strong therapeutic relationship (Geller & Greenberg, 2002; Hayes & Vinca, 2011). Further research found that successful therapeutic outcomes increased when clients experienced their therapist as being more therapeutically present in session (Geller, Greenberg, & Watson, 2010). The ability to be therapeutically present in session is like a muscle that can be trained (Austin & Austin, 2018; Geller, 2017). The operational definition of therapeutic presence should be scaffolded into students' education. We have created a definition geared more toward beginning counseling students, which identifies therapeutic presence as

> the way in which students use their self-awareness, awareness of their client, and their awareness of the therapeutic relationship to sense what is needed from moment to moment during session. Once students sense what is needed in a moment, they intentionally use their awareness and skills therapeutically to facilitate their client's healing in that moment (Austin & Austin, 2018, p. 493).

As students work toward building their therapeutically present muscles in session, their understanding of therapeutic presence may fit with a more advanced definition of therapeutic presence developed by Geller and Greenberg (2002), who defined therapeutic presence as more than being congruent, real, accepting, empathetic, or responsive; it "involves bringing one's whole self into the encounter with the client, being completely in the moment on a multiplicity of levels, physically, emotionally, cognitively and spiritually" (pp. 82–83).

Learning to be therapeutically present encapsulates the offered conditions (Rogers, 1951) and the skills, knowledge, and attitudes identified by the CACREP. We discuss ways to train students to be more therapeutically present throughout the book. For more information about therapeutic presence, refer to Austin and Austin (2018), Geller (2017), Geller and Porges (2014), and Colosimo and Pos (2015).

The Role of the Counselor Educator in the Classroom

It is largely your responsibility to help students develop the previously mentioned skills, knowledge, and attitudes required to do effective counseling and pass their licensure exams. In the classroom, we do this by creating an environment that facilitates learning. This process must be flexible to meet a wide variety of students' needs. This task will require all of you—your identity, education, classroom experience, and clinical experience.

Eriksen and McAuliffe (2001) offered suggestions for counselor educators finding their role in the classroom, including the following: (a) encourage expression of conflict, (b) show commitment in the face of doubt, (c) question categorical thinking, (d) process interpersonal dynamics and metacognition awareness, (e) personalize teaching, (f) value and promote experience, (g) vary structure, and (h) emphasize multiple perspectives.

To follow their suggestions, the therapeutic relationship between you and your students must be strong. Trust is the key ingredient of a classroom that is willing to be vulnerable enough to confront one another. Trust is especially needed when processing interpersonal dynamics and metacognitions. The role of the counselor educator is explored in greater depth throughout the book. Practical examples of how to follow Eriksen and McAuliffe's (2001) suggestions are also discussed throughout the following chapters.

Developing the Syllabus

The syllabus, like the intake paperwork during an initial counseling session, may be the first chance students get to build a strong relationship with you and the course. It needs to be written for and to the students, not at the students. By now, you may already know the general purpose of a syllabus. It is essentially a road map for the course, which includes an introduction to the course, the schedule, class assignments, readings, and activities. However, most universities or colleges have their own unique structure, policies, and verbiage that must be included. In addition to these must-haves, some programs want you to display learning outcomes, policy statements, as well as CACREP standards and key performance indicators. In some cases, typically in clinical courses, the syllabus serves as an informed consent document or a contract that both students and professors honor. In fact, after Jude served on a grievance committee, most issues were resolved after the committee looked at and interpreted the course's syllabus. It is important to be intentional when creating and following a syllabus.

A syllabus is typically 5 to 10 pages long depending upon the attachments you may need to include, such as rubrics or assignment examples. According to Grunert (1997), some learning-centered syllabi stretch up to 30 to 50 pages. This type of syllabi includes things such as notetaking, readings, study material, writing style suggestions, and/or exam study guide information. Syllabi should be tailored to fit the class. While we cannot give you an example of a universal syllabus because each program and university are unique, we can provide suggestions to consider when formulating or updating your course syllabus. The following are essential syllabus items:

- Your name, title, office hours, location, contact information, and a professional website. If students cannot meet face-to-face, provide personal cell phone numbers or video calling options. We encourage caution when providing students with personal contact information. Place limitations around contacting you using personal numbers by outlining specific days and hours you will answer. This can potentially stop students from contacting you 24-7.
- Course information such as meeting times and location, required and suggested texts, any materials needed, links to specific videos, or the course LMS (learning management system).
- A detailed description of the course assignments. This is probably one of the most important elements of the syllabus. As students, we bypassed everything and looked for the assignments. The more details added into the description of the assignments can decrease the questions from students. We also add specifics about our expectations. For example, we have added specifics about page limits on

written assignments—even going far enough to take off percentage points for papers longer than the requirement. Outline ungraded assignments such as practice quizzes or paper drafts. If you plan to grade class participation, your expectations for participation need to be outlined as well.

- Student learning outcomes need to be outlined. They are a list of things your students should be able to do by the end of the course. As students, we did not care about these outcomes, but they are important to us as faculty because often our teacher evaluations are tied to these learning outcomes. More than outlining them in the syllabus, they should be discussed in class throughout the semester.
- A breakdown of the grading scale and the weight of each assignment's grade on the course grade needs to be outlined. Explain the grading system with percentage breakdowns.
- Explanation of policies regarding late work, revisions, or failure to submit work.
- Policies on attendance and tardiness should be outlined. We found this to be particularly important in clinical skills classes that students need to attend so that all students can have opportunities to participate.
- Academic honesty policy should be outlined and also how you plan to check written work for plagiarism. Some universities provide ways to do this via the course's online shell.
- Your university may require you to outline their policies on Americans with Disabilities Act (ADA) accommodations. Students may reach out to discuss their specific accommodations and would like to personalize their experience in the course.

- A section outlining classroom culture, professionalism, and academic discourse. When working with a new cohort, we sometimes dedicate a piece of the first class to discussing what it means to be a graduate student. We discuss the difference between undergraduate and graduate classrooms and their role in creating a safe learning environment, defining what a safe classroom is, and things students can do to avoid making other students uncomfortable.
- A detailed, week-by-week course schedule identifying the topics, readings, and assignments due on each day.

Assessments: Students' Learning and Your Performance

There are two different kinds of assessments: summative and formative evaluations. Summative evaluations happen at the end of a semester, whereas formative evaluations occur before the end so that we can practice and refine the curriculum before the summative evaluation. According to Lau (2016), one is not better than the other. Creating a system where they work together is ideal. The combination of the two evaluations are more effective if the assessments are connected to each other and the learning process, students buy into the learning process and want to improve, and the relationship is strong between students and professor. The goal of assessments is to facilitate and track learning. In this evaluation process, clearly defined and discussed learning objectives are vital to receiving useful feedback about the course. There is a greater discussion regarding course and program evaluations, including ways to evaluate learning and performance in each course, throughout the book.

SUMMARY

In our lives as counselor educators, we assume many roles and responsibilities. These roles and responsibilities can make it feel like we are working 24-7. There is always a student emailing at 3:00 a.m., or a book chapter due, or a deadline to meet, or accreditation to prepare for, or students to meet. When entering our first faculty positions, feelings of unpreparedness, fear, and incongruence overwhelmed us. It can sometimes feel like students smell fear and the classroom environment focuses our inadequacies to a sharp edge for 6 to 9 hours a week. Effectively managing these roles and responsibilities comes with experience, with more experience comes different roles and responsibilities, and the cycle continues. Within these role and responsibilities, counselor educators have a unique opportunity to impact their communities through one interaction with a student. One moment of genuine sharing of a clinical thought can have a positive ripple effect in the lives of our students' clients. Our hope is that in this chapter you saw the challenges and potential of this profession. We go into greater detail regarding the topics discussed in this chapter throughout the book.

REFERENCES

Aliakbari, M., & Faraji, E. (2011). Basic principles of critical pedagogy. Second international conference on humanities, historical and social sciences. *IPEDR, 17*, 78–85. Retrieved from http://www.ipedr.com/vol17/14-CHHSS%202011-H00057.pdf

Altbach, P. G. (2015). The Carnegie classification of American higher education: More—and less—than meets the eye. *International Higher Education*, (80), 21–23. doi:10.6017/ihe.2015.80.6153

Ambrose, S. A., Bridges, M. W., DiPietro, M., Lovett, M. C., & Norman, M. K. (2010). *How learning works: Seven research-based principles for smart teaching.* San Francisco, CA: John Wiley & Sons.

Association for Counselor Education and Supervision. (n.d.). *About ACES.* Retrieved from https://acesonline.net/about-aces

Association for Counselor Education and Supervision. (1979). *Standards for preparation in counselor education.* Falls Church, VA: American Personnel and Guidance Association.

Association for Counselor Education and Supervision. (2014). *Statement on educational standards for counselor licensure.* Alexandria, VA: Author

Austin, J. T., & Austin, J. A. (2018). Initial exploration of therapeutic presence pedagogy in counselor education. *International Journal for the Advancement of Counselling, 40,* 481–500. doi:10.1007/s10447-018-9339-x

Baldwin, M. (2013). *The use of self in therapy.* New York, NY: Routledge.

Baltrinic, E. R., Jencius, M., & McGlothlin, J. (2016). Coteaching in counselor education: Preparing doctoral students for future teaching. *Counselor Education and Supervision, 55*(1), 31–45. doi:10.1002/ceas.12031

Barkley, E. F., & Major, C. H. (2018). *Interactive lecturing: A handbook for college faculty.* San Francisco, CA: John Wiley & Sons.

Barrio Minton, C. A., Wachter Morris, C. A., & Yaites, L. D. (2014). Pedagogy in counselor education: A 10-year content analysis of journals. *Counselor Education and Supervision, 53*(3), 162–177. doi:10.1002/j.1556-6978.2014.00055.x

Bjork, R. A. (2017). Creating desirable difficulties to enhance learning. In I. Wallace & L. Kirkman (Eds.), *Best of the best: Progress* (pp. 81–85). Carmarthen, UK: Crown House Publishing.

Bransford, J. D., Brown, A. L., & Cocking, R. R. (Eds.). (2000). *How people learn* (Vol. 11). Washington, DC: National Academies Press.

Colosimo, K. A., & Pos, A. E. (2015). A rational model of expressed therapeutic presence. *Journal of Psychotherapy Integration, 25*(2), 100–114. doi:10.1037/a0038879

Council for Accreditation of Counseling and Related Educational Programs. (2001). *2001 standards.* Alexandria, VA: Author.

Council for Accreditation of Counseling and Related Educational Programs. (2009). *2009 standards*. Alexandria, VA: Author.

Council for Accreditation of Counseling and Related Educational Programs. (2015a). *2016 CACREP standards*. Retrieved from http://www.cacrep.org/wp-content/uploads/2017/08/2016-Standards-with-citations.pdf

Council for Accreditation of Counseling and Related Educational Programs. (2015b). *About CACREP*. Retrieved from https://www.cacrep.org/about-cacrep

Council for Accreditation of Counseling and Related Educational Programs. (2020). *About CACREP*. Retrieved from https://www.cacrep.org/about-cacrep/

Duncan, B. L., Miller, S. D., Wampold, B. E., & Hubble, M. A. (2010). *The heart and soul of change: Delivering what works in therapy*. Washington, DC: American Psychological Association.

Elliott, A., Salazar, B. M., Dennis, B. L., Bohecker, L., Nielson, T., LaMantia, K., & Kleist, D. M. (2019). Pedagogical perspectives on counselor education: An autoethnographic experience of doctoral student development. *The Qualitative Report, 24*(4), 648–666. Retrieved from https://nsuworks.nova.edu/tqr/vol24/iss4/2

Eriksen, K., & McAuliffe, G. (Eds.). (2001). *Teaching counselors and therapists: Constructivist and developmental course design*. Westport, CT: Bergin & Garvey/Greenwood.

Freire, P. (2018). *Pedagogy of the oppressed*. New York, NY: Bloomsbury Publishing.

Geller, S. M. (2017). *A practical guide to cultivating therapeutic presence*. Washington, DC: American Psychological Association.

Geller, S. M., & Greenberg, L. S. (2002). Therapeutic presence: Therapists' experience of presence in the psychotherapy encounter. *Person-Centered and Experiential Psychotherapies, 1*(1–2), 71–86. doi:10.1080/14779757.2002.9688279

Geller, S. M., Greenberg, L. S., & Watson, J. G. (2010). Therapist and client perceptions of therapeutic presence: The development of a measure. *Psychotherapy Research, 20*(5), 599–610. doi:10.1080/10503307.2010.495957

Geller, S. M., & Porges, S. W. (2014). Therapeutic presence: Neurophysiological mechanisms mediating feeling safe in therapeutic relationships. *Journal of Psychotherapy Integration, 24*(3), 178–188. doi:10.1037/a0037511

Gregg, G. S. (2017). *Social values and moral intuitions: The world-views of "millennial" young adults.* New York, NY: Routledge.

Grunert, J. (1997). *The course syllabus: A learning-centered approach.* Bolton, MA: Anker Publishing Company.

Hayes, J., & Vinca, J. (2011). *Therapist presence and its relationship to empathy, session, depth, and symptom reduction.* Bern, Switzerland: Society for Psychotherapy Research.

Knowles, M. S. (1970). Gearing adult education for the seventies. *The Journal of Continuing Education in Nursing, 1*(1), 11–16. Retrieved from https://eric.ed.gov/?id=EJ024167

Lau, A. M. S. (2016). 'Formative good, summative bad?'–A review of the dichotomy in assessment literature. *Journal of Further and Higher Education, 40*(4), 509–525. doi:10.1080/0309877X.2014.984600

Magnuson, S. (2002). New assistant professors of counselor education: Their 1st year. *Counselor Education and Supervision, 41*(4), 306–320. doi:10.1002/j.1556-6978.2002.tb01293.x

Malott, K. M., Hall, K. H., Sheely-Moore, A., Krell, M. M., & Cardaciotto, L. (2014). Evidence-based teaching in higher education: Application to counselor education. *Counselor Education and Supervision, 53*(4), 294–305. doi:10.1002/j.1556-6978.2014.00064.x

McAuliffe, G., & Eriksen, K. (Eds.). (2011). *Handbook of counselor preparation: Constructivist, developmental, and experiential approaches.* Thousand Oaks, CA: Sage.

Mezirow, J. (2018). Transformative learning theory. In K. Illeris (Ed.), *Contemporary theories of learning: Learning theorists* (pp. 114–128). New York, NY: Routledge.

Nixon-Ponder, S. (1995). Using problem-posing dialogue: In adult literacy education. *Adult Learning, 7*(2), 10–12. Retrieved from https://www.researchgate.net/publication/234598591_Using_Problem-Posing_Dialogue_In_Adult_Literacy_Education

Okech, J. E. A., & Rubel, D. J. (Eds.). (2018). *Counselor education in the 21st century: Issues and experiences.* San Francisco, CA: John Wiley & Sons.

Orr, J. J., Hall, S. F., & Hulse-Killacky, D. (2008). A model for collaborative teaching teams in counselor education.

Counselor Education and Supervision, 47(3), 146–163. doi:10.1002/j.1556-6978.2008.tb00046.x

Palmer, P. J. (2017). *The courage to teach: Exploring the inner landscape of a teacher's life*. San Francisco, CA: John Wiley & Sons.

Rogers, C. R. (1951). *Client-centered therapy*. Boston, MA: Houghton Mifflin.

Skovholt, T. M., & Ronnestad, M. H. (1992). Themes in therapist and counselor development. *Journal of Counseling and Development, 70*(4), 505–515. doi:10.1002/j.1556-6676.1992.tb01646.x

Stewart, K. D., & Bernhardt, P. C. (2010). Comparing Millennials to pre-1987 students and with one another. *North American Journal of Psychology, 12*(3), 579–602. Retrieved from https://www.researchgate.net/publication/230683045_Comparing_Millennials_to_pre-1987_students_and_with_one_another

Sweller, J. (2016). Cognitive load theory, evolutionary educational psychology, and instructional design. In D. Geary & D. Berch (Eds.), *Evolutionary perspectives on child development and education* (pp. 291–306). Cham, Switzerland: Springer Publishing Company.

Vijaya Kumari, S. N. (2014). Constructivist approach to teacher education: An integrative model for reflective teaching. *Journal on Educational Psychology, 7*(4), 31–40. doi:10.26634/jpsy.7.4.2655

Whitman, J. S., & Beeson, E. T. (2018). Developing a personal philosophy of teaching. In L. R. Haddock & J. S. Whitman (Eds.), *Preparing the educator in counselor education* (pp. 26–46). New York, NY: Routledge.

Wilson, K., & Korn, J. H. (2007). Attention during lectures: Beyond ten minutes. *Teaching of Psychology, 34*(2), 85–89. doi:10.1080/00986280701291291

Wlodkowski, R. J., & Ginsberg, M. B. (2017). *Enhancing adult motivation to learn: A comprehensive guide for teaching all adults*. Hoboken, NJ: John Wiley & Sons.

2 | ORIENTATION TO PROFESSIONAL COUNSELING COURSES

INTRODUCTION

The orientation course in counseling programs is called many names: Introduction to Counseling, Orientation to the Profession, or Becoming a Professional Counselor. Regardless of the name, these courses are content heavy and are often placed at the beginning of the student's journey. The course provides a comprehensive overview of the entire profession. Counselor educators cover roughly 100 years of important historical events, individuals, theories, philosophies, laws, social movements, research, licensure, specialties, and more related to the counseling profession. They also cover future trends, such as social justice issues, technology, social media, politics, and other future directions of our profession.

This chapter, like the others to follow, breaks down this content-heavy course. Important topics covered in this course are discussed. A brief review of the recent pertinent literature is examined. Also discussed are different approaches to prepare and teach this course. We share our personal experience when teaching this course. Lastly, course assignments used to cover important topics are described.

COURSE DESCRIPTION

The standard Council for Accreditation of Counseling and Related Educational Programs (CACREP) syllabus for this course might describe it as an introduction to the theory, practice, methods, basic principles, and concepts used by counselors in educational, community, and clinical settings. It may go on to explain that the purpose of this course is to have students gain an overview of the counseling profession through class discussion, readings, papers, exams, and experiential activities.

While this is all true, it masks the volume of information students will need to grasp throughout this course. To be fair, teaching this course feels like drinking out of a fire hose. In many respects, this course summarizes 4 years of an undergraduate degree in psychology. The title of the course could be Counseling From 1900 to 2097, because counselor educators also attempt to cover topics that students may face by the time they graduate.

When trying to cover the large amount of information, it is important for counselor educators to be mindful that in this course, students work to see themselves as a counselor. This course may be the first earnest step toward the counselor's chair. In some respects, this class can serve as an informed consent for students who are on the fence about what they are getting themselves into. Each week, a different part of the profession is covered. Counselor educators who can present the good, the bad, and the ugly sides of the counseling profession may better help students make an informed choice about continuing their education. Presenting these sides of the profession to students can be like teaching a child about their ancestry. Counselor educators lay out how the field has become what it is today.

This class is important because it provides students with a full perspective of the profession. Before students know where they are going, they must first internalize where the profession came from. This process of internalizing information is another critical element of this class. Undergraduate classrooms can tend to be knowledge based. Students who study hard to retain the information have a better chance of succeeding. Graduate counselor training programs ask more of their students. While this class is information dense, it still asks students to develop the appropriate skills and attitudes of the profession. To ensure this, some counselor educators teaching this course use the early classes to orientate students to graduate school. Facilitating discussions about how to survive and thrive during counselor training can set the stage for students to internalize the information presented, not just memorize it.

COURSE OBJECTIVES

The course has standard objects, which are found in most CACREP accredited programs. For example, by the end of the Orientation to the Profession course, students will be able to compare and contrast counselors with psychologists, psychiatrists, social workers, psychotherapists, and life coaches. Students will be able to distinguish the various counseling specialty areas, such as school counseling, mental health counseling, community counseling, counseling in student affairs, and marriage and family counseling. Students will examine the historical roots of counseling and examine its relationship to the historical roots of psychology, psychiatry, and social work. Students will learn about three standards in the profession: ethics, accreditation, and credentialing. Students will be introduced to counseling theories, counseling practices, family counseling, career counseling, group dynamics, group process, consultation, physical psychosocial models of development, abnormal psychology, the *Diagnostic and Statistical Manual of Mental Disorders*, psychotropic medication, psychological assessment, and psychological research. In this class, students will examine how multicultural issues, ethical issues, and professional issues permeate counseling.

In addition to these course objectives, students learn about the many career options for counselors today. More and more, counselors are choosing to take nontraditional routes to serve their communities. Whether students are interested in wilderness therapy or distance therapy, this course can offer a platform for students to workshop their ideas. We often set aside time during each class period to process students' career questions. Instead of rejecting ideas as unrealistic, we take time to discuss the ethical and legal ramifications for their choices and career goals.

Students also walk away from the course with a realistic idea of what being a therapist looks like for themselves and their families. Students can process what goes through a counselor's mind when a client walks in. Using personal experiences, students visualize themselves in our counselor's chair as they try to keep up with a client in crisis, or an arguing couple.

Additionally, students will take away an understanding of how important it is to fully contextualize a client. Students at this stage of their development may not be able to hold both a life-span perspective and a theoretical perspective. However, presenting these perspectives and talking through mock cases from these lenses facilitates their growth.

Another important objective of this course in addition to the standard CACREP objectives is for students to explore their licensure process. Students walk away from this class with an understanding of what it takes to obtain licensure in their discipline and state. They have a chance to look through the state licensure board website, download the paperwork, discuss supervision, and explore postgraduate internships or other forms of accruing clinical hours.

These objectives cover a large area of topics within the counseling profession. Covering these topics gives students an in-depth orientation to the profession they are about to enter. To achieve these objects, several topics must be covered throughout the course of the semester. At times it can feel like counselor educators are teaching an entirely different course each class period. Following are a list and brief description of the must-cover topics in this course.

MUST-COVER TOPICS

What Is Counseling?

In 2005, 31 counseling organizations formed a collaborative committee that aimed to create a definition of counseling. They called their project "20/20: A Vision for the Future of Counseling." The 20/20 committee provided the following definition of counseling: "Counseling is a professional relationship that empowers diverse individuals, families, and groups to accomplish mental health, wellness, education, and career goals" (Kaplan, Tarvydas, & Gladding, 2014, p. 368). According to Erford (2017), the committee embedded within this definition five important elements:

1. Counseling is a profession that requires graduate-level education; necessitates adherence to ethical standards; and encourages licensure, certification, and organizational membership and involvement.
2. Counseling is holistic and concerns itself with treating the entire person—without stepping outside one's area of competence.
3. Counseling focuses on relatively healthy-functioning individuals who are having trouble.

4. Counseling is empirically driven and based on theoretically sound underpinnings and interventions.
5. Counseling involves the facilitation of behavioral, cognitive, and emotional change.

In addition to covering this empirically founded definition of counseling, it is important to focus on the aspects of counseling that are more difficult to define. One such quality is therapeutic presence. Students often confuse being present in session with the ability of being therapeutically present with clients. While it is confusing, researchers such as Shari Geller, Leslie Greenberg, and Austin and Austin (2018) have attempted to further explain the difference. In short, when students traditionally think of "presence," they see it as a noun, a way of being in session. Therapeutic presence is a verb; it is a way of doing therapy. Geller and Greenberg (2002) concretized the definition of therapeutic presence for clinicians when they described it as "bringing one's whole self into the encounter with the client, being completely in the moment on a multiplicity of levels, physically, emotionally, cognitively and spiritually" (pp. 82–83). Later, Geller, Greenberg, and Watson (2010) found that therapy was more effective when clients experienced their therapist as being therapeutically present in session. We continued this line of research, focusing on counseling student development of therapeutic presence. We aimed our definition of therapeutic presence and examples of how to develop it at students' developmental level. We found that for students, therapeutic presence is the way in which they use their self-awareness, awareness of their client, and their awareness of the therapeutic relationship to sense what is needed from moment to moment during a session. Once students sense what is needed in a moment, they intentionally use their awareness and skills therapeutically to facilitate their client's healing in that moment. Therapeutic presence is an umbrella concept that encapsulates attunement, relational courage, and other aspects of the therapeutic process that seem intangible.

Covering these intangible elements of the therapeutic process helps students develop an understanding of the art of counseling. As they matriculate through the program, taking technique, diagnosis, assessment, and other technical courses, students can lose sight of what works in therapy: building a genuine connection with the clients (Duncan, Miller, Wampold, & Hubble, 2010). As those authors explained, a strong therapeutic relationship is the heart and soul of change in therapy. Each student has his or her own unique characteristics that influence the therapeutic process. The art of therapy is becoming aware of those characteristics and knowing when and how to use them in session. Although the techniques, diagnoses, assessments, and other technical aspects of counseling are important, sometimes change happens during silence, or a well-timed joke. It is important in this class to help students begin the process of figuring out their counselor identity.

Counselor Identity

Despite the many topics covered throughout this course, students will not leave with a full and complete understanding of who they are as counselors. Each student goes through a unique journey to find himself or herself in the *chair*. This journey can take years and includes a process of engaging with values, attitudes, biases, family of origin, relational dynamics, multicultural issues, and other personal growth actions. Perhaps covering this topic as a journey instead of a destination is more effective.

Skovholt and Ronnestad (1992) identified 20 themes and eight stages of counselor development. Each stage has a central task and learning process. Brott and Myers (1999) went on to discuss the development professional school counselor identity. Both models present the growth process as being on a continuum. Helping students view their identity development from these continuums can put their work into perspective.

History

What does it mean to know oneself as a counselor? It means that counselors have a firm understanding of where the counseling profession has come from and their role in its future. To set this firm understanding, counselor educators teaching this course must cover the people, issues, and societal forces that shaped the counseling profession. In most textbooks for this course there exists a counseling timeline that identifies some of the important events throughout the history of the profession. Some of the key events to cover are the following:

- Frank Parsons founded the Vocational Bureau of the Civic Services House in 1908.
- Sigmund Freud presented his psychoanalytic approach in the United States in 1909.
- Psychological instruments were used to screen solders during World War I in 1914.
- The Army Alpha and Beta tests were created for the military in 1917.
- Child-guidance clinics were created in 1921.
- Group therapy was used by Alfred Adler in 1922.
- Edward Strong Jr. developed the Strong Vocational Interest Blank in 1927.
- The first family and marriage counseling center opened in New York City in 1929.
- Counselors were used extensively during World War II in 1939.
- Individuals could receive a certification in School Counseling in 1940.

- Client-centered therapy was introduced when Carl Rogers published *Counseling and Psychotherapy* in 1942.
- Other counseling theories flourished in 1950.
- The American Personnel and Guidance Association, known now as the American Counseling Association, formed in 1952.
- Mental health centers were built due to the enactment of the Community Mental Health Centers Act in 1963.
- The Civil Rights Act was passed in 1964.
- Many national counseling associations were chartered starting in 1965.
- Who could provide counseling services were restricted due to legislation proposed by the American Counseling Association in 1967.
- The Family Educational Rights and Privacy Act was passed by Congress in 1974.
- The CACREP was founded in 1981.
- The National Board of Certified Counselors was established in 1983.
- The International Association of Marriage and Family Counselors was chartered in 1989.
- By 2001, more than 31,000 counselors held the Nationally Certified Counselor certification.
- The 20/20 committee endorsed a definition of counseling in 2011.
- In 2015, the Council on Rehabilitation Education (CORE) and CACREP merged.

Future

The counseling profession has an illustrious past, filled with small individual efforts that made a big impact. The future of the counseling profession is filled with opportunities and challenges. Some of the challenges facing the counseling profession include outcome research and evidence-based practices, increased diversity within the communities we serve, technology, advocacy, leadership, professional divisiveness, and gatekeeping.

Evidence-Based Practices, Research-Based Practices, and Outcomes Research. The counseling field is attempting to close the gap between practice and research. Practitioners are encouraged to research and vice versa. This could potentially provide more empirical support for counseling interventions. Counseling students need to be trained to do research and/or understand the methodology enough to apply the findings to their work with clients.

Managed Care. Regardless of a counselor educator's opinions regarding the managed care system, students need a basic understanding of it. Essentially, the current system is both good and bad for clinicians and clients. The system attempts to provide accountability and consistent work opportunities for counselors. However, the system also lowers the amount of sessions clients can receive. Clinicians face a number of pressures within this system to provide the best care for the client's coverage.

Multiculturalism, Diversity, and Social Justice Counseling. Counseling interventions have been normed and validated to serve predominantly White, male, educated, middle-class populations (Erford, 2017). The multicultural movement in counseling aims to change this by emphasizing more diverse perspectives.

Technology. Technology is being used in counseling for supervision, clinical work, consultations, counselor education, and much more. While technology can offer benefits for clinicians and clients, there are also elements of this topic that can cause harm. Students who choose to use technology in their practice need to learn how to do so ethically.

Professional Advocacy and Social Advocacy Counseling. According to Lee (2018), there are many ways for clinicians to advocate for the profession, their clients, and the larger communities served. He went on to suggest that the goal of professional advocacy is to create equality with other helping professions and social advocacy is aimed at doing the same between our clients and the societies where they exist.

Licensure Portability. This refers to counselors' ability to travel from state to state and retain their ability to practice counseling in their new state. Although no portability agreement has been reached, states with equivalent licensure requirements often accept each other's clinicians after those clinicians pay the new state's fees.

Crisis Prevention. At this point in students' training, they need to be introduced to the basic frameworks for assessing crisis situations in session, specifically suicide assessments. Students may take an entire course focused on crisis and trauma. An introduction in this course may allow them to discuss their concerns and fears before they face clients in crisis.

In the following sections, we discuss our personal experiences teaching this course. Our way is not *the* way, but *a* way. We hope that our discussion will spark ideas for your semester as you prepare to teach the Professional Orientation course.

PERSONAL EXPERIENCE

Teaching Approach

When approaching this course, we strongly consider the following:

 a. The Professional Orientation course could be the student's first graduate-level course.
 b. Students will have questions as they enter the profession.
 c. There is a great amount of content that needs to be covered in this course.

d. Students will have an entire curriculum dedicated to the specific topics covered in this course.

This course serves as an orientation to graduate learning, which is different from undergraduate education. Graduate students take more responsibility for their education than undergraduate students do. In many cases, information known increases competence, and competence increases earning potential. Although counseling as a profession appears altruistic, counselors have bills they need to pay just as much as clients do. Students do not need to take a vow of poverty to work in this profession. Discussing this potential correlation prepares students to have a different relationship to the information covered in graduate courses. We often show students the websites of other clinicians in the area so they get a picture of the professional atmosphere they are entering. Students tend to see clinicians and agencies as ones after whom they want to model their careers and where they want to work. It makes life after the degree tangible, helping students to see the light at the end of the tunnel.

In addition to gaining a postgraduate school perspective, this course offers students a chance to learn and write like graduate students. The knowledge needs to be flexible, so students cannot just take in information to pass quizzes and exams. They must be able to adapt their knowledge to different circumstances. In some cases, a client's life may depend upon how well they can flex their knowledge. Additionally, writing is more technical and diverse. This course may require students to write multiple 10-page papers where one is research focused and the other is personal. Graduate students are required to articulate their ideas and perspectives professionally. This prepares them to one day write a letter to a judge on behalf of a client. There are several differences between undergraduate and graduate schools. Helping students to connect their course work to their careers helps them to thrive within this course and the counseling program.

Because this could be student's first graduate course, counselor educators can expect students to have many questions. These questions are aimed at a variety of subjects, most of which are covered throughout the course schedule. It is beneficial to provide students a space in class to process through their questions. The topic of the day can focus the discussion on a part of the counseling profession. By creating this culture during each class, students can read and prepare their questions. This Socratic format breaks the class up so that counselor educators are not lecturing at students for 3 hours. Due to the amount of content counselor educators are expected to cover in this course, it is tempting to create a 70-slide PowerPoint presentation and read directly from it.

As stated earlier, the amount of content covered in this course is overwhelming. Students need to build a relationship with the content and integrate it into their way of being. We have found that a concise and organized PowerPoint presentation, in addition to the assigned reading, provides students with the essential content needed to support their growth. When preparing a concise PowerPoint, we consider what topics from the readings students might want to focus on in class. We avoid creating a PowerPoint presentation with 40 or more slides that merely summarize the information read by students the night before class. Instead, we attempt to spend 2 hours of a 3-hour class covering content and the last hour filled with discussion. If each slide took 5 to 10 minutes to cover, we would create 15 to 20 slides each lecture. Typically, images, graphs, videos, or short sentences cover the PowerPoint slides. Furthermore, detailed and expansive lecture notes cover all of the content placed on the PowerPoint slides. This helps to avoid overcrowding PowerPoint slides with paragraphs of text that bore students. The information not on the PowerPoint slides can be found within the lecture notes.

Giving students access to lecture notes can take the pressure off counselor educators who feel the need to cover every detail of the textbook. In addition, understanding that students will have entire courses dedicated to each daily topic covered in the Professional Orientation course can relieve pressure for counselor educators. Focusing on merely orientating students to the profession may be less overwhelming for students and counselor educators.

Student Experience

According to Guo, Klein, and Ro (2019), students' learning outcomes are affected by student interest, self-efficacy, and their perception of the instructor. There is a butterfly effect in counseling programs; counselor educators influence student development, and then student development influences client therapeutic outcomes. Often, the limitations of counselor educators affect the outcomes of students' therapy sessions. Counselor educators need to be aware of how students experience them in class because they model for them what it means to be a counselor. Here, we briefly share how students expressed experiencing us in class.

Students experience us as having a nonanxious presence in this course. Students enter this course with a certain level of anxiety. This anxiety often gets in the way of student learning. We attempt to help students settle into the class by settling ourselves in as soon as possible. Students also experience us as open and accepting of their questions and ideas. As stated earlier, a considerable amount of this course's class periods is spent in discussion. We want to create a space for students to feel safe enough to share ideas or ask questions that they may be embarrassed to express. Students also experience us as genuine. During discussions, we share our personal experiences as students and as clinicians. One of the benefits of being young professors is that we were in our students' shoes a couple of years ago. We can talk about how we experience topics that are covered in class, and our experiences may not be too far removed from our students' experience. Students build cohort bonds during this course as they discuss ideas and questions. Cultivating these bonds are a secondary benefit for their development.

Course Preparation

This course takes a considerable amount of planning. If counselor educators plan to host guest speakers, therapists, social workers, psychologists, and other types of helpers need at least 1- to 2-month heads-up before speaking in this course. Lecture notes, readings, presentations, videos, classroom activities, and other experiences need to be well thought out and organized before class begins. Here, we briefly share our experience preparing for this course.

If the course is scheduled for Thursdays from 2:30 to 5:50 p.m. and today is Monday, we would start preparing on Monday. This would give us about 4 days to prepare. We would start by rereading the book chapters assigned for Thursday's class, highlighting and making notes for the lecture. If we were planning to host a guest speaker in class, we would check in with him or her to confirm his or her appearance. We would then start to create detailed lecture notes with links to videos and additional information not found in the book. After completing the lecture notes, we would reread the chapter, paying close attention to the essential points. These key points are added to the PowerPoint lecture we create. After creating the presentation, we create 10 to 15 process questions to discuss as a group in the last hour of class. Sometimes students will pose their own discussion questions during the lecture.

A challenge when preparing for this course is boiling down the content to the information most pertinent to students' training. As we mentioned earlier, we attempt to present the course content clearly and concisely so it is easy for students to internalize. It is difficult to decide which key historical point to focus on in class or which evidence-based research article to present. We often address this challenge by inviting students to share their curiosities regarding the next class's topic. Their comments direct our focus when preparing for the next class.

Nuts and Bolts

The nuts and bolts of this course involve managing time during each class period, overseeing the amount of written assignments, using the course's online platform to enhance student experience, and being mindful of the multicultural considerations. These elements are the technical parts of counselor education. This section briefly covers some of these parts.

This course devours class time. Hours feel like minutes because of the amount of content that needs to be covered. To help manage the time in class, we present students with an outline of the class period, hour by hour, before the lecture begins. We explain the class objective and what we hope to cover. Graduate students can help move the class along because they get an idea of the information we must cover during that class period.

Then, the clock becomes our greatest tool. We create our lectures around the 2 hours we have allotted. This means that we aim to spend about 10 minutes per topic or PowerPoint slide. We choose 12 to 15 topics to focus the lecture. Then we choose five to six discussion questions to focus the last hour of the class. Our understanding that students may take an entire course on that day's class topic helps us maintain our perspective of orientating students to these topics. We carefully watch the time and gently move the conversation from one topic to the next.

In addition to managing the time while in class, counselor educators in this course may find themselves grading 300 to 360 pages in student assignments. One of the ways we address this challenge is to train students to write well. We take some time early in the semester to discuss the American Psychological Association (APA) Style of writing and the assignment rubrics. We then review these points a week before writing assignments are due. Prepared students may make less technical errors in the papers, significantly decreasing the corrections and feedback needed.

An additional technical element of this course is managing the online course resources such as Canvas, Blackboard, Moodle, or other platforms. In this course, the online platform can serve as a repository for files such as PowerPoint presentations, soft copies of handouts, daily quizzes, lecture notes, and other documents students may need throughout the course of the semester. We also use these online platforms to communicate with students about the class, post links to videos, and keep track of the grading system. Organization is key. Students cannot use what they cannot find. Online platforms are particularly helpful in this course when counselor educators create modules for each topic that host documents, videos, and other pertinent information. This can help students mentally organize this information and plan for each class. A well-organized online platform can be students' safe harbor when the semester starts to feel overwhelming.

Lastly, counselor educators teaching this course have an opportunity to juxtapose the development of counseling as a profession with important cultural occurrences. For example, the segregation of African Americans in America occurred for approximately 89 years from 1865 to 1954. As stated earlier, the American Personnel and Guidance Association, known now as the American Counseling Association, formed in 1952. Counseling theories and approaches were developed before the American Personnel and Guidance Association formed; client-centered therapy was introduced when Carl Rogers published *Counseling and Psychotherapy* in 1942. Knowing these professional events, and the cultural environment, through counseling's development, makes for interesting conversation in class. African Americans and other people of color may not see themselves reflected in the profession, in theories, textbooks, or even their faculty. It is important that counselor educators address these multicultural issues in class.

Advice

Teaching this course is challenging and rewarding. A rewarding aspect of this course is the discussion hour at the end of every class. Dedicating an hour each class to processing the topic of the day in more depth allows counselor educators to build a relationship with the students that supports their learning. It is also enjoyable to watch students grow into the idea of counseling as a profession as opposed to it being an idea. One of the first noticeable changes is the types of questions students ask. They may start by distantly asking about what counselors in general can and cannot do. Then, a couple of weeks into the semester, when students feel comfortable, they may start asking specific questions about their careers. It allows counselor educators to know their students on a personal level. As they share their hopes and plans, counselor educators can tailor lectures to fit the needs of their students.

While teaching this course can be rewarding, there are pitfalls to be mindful of when preparing to teach it. The amount of content covered in this course can cause some counselor educators to teach at a distance. Creating a cold presentation with all the book information on various slides is easy but may not address students' needs. Another pitfall is not respecting the process each class period. Part of what makes this course great is that students can talk through different topics, their ideas, frustrations with the profession, and career plans. Respect this process by being nonjudgmental, creating a safe environment, and managing class time well. This course may be one of the few courses where students have less responsibility and pressure when discussing the profession and how they fit into it.

If we were teaching this course for the first time, we would do the following:

- Prepare guest speakers well in advance
- Create well-organized and easy-to-follow rubrics for each assignment
- Put together a writing tips presentation for students to refer back to when needed
- Teach the course relationally rather than impersonally
- Use the online course platform to help students keep up with the readings and notes
- Remain mindful that this course may be students' first graduate-level course
- Not avoid discussing the frustrations and disappointments experienced by clients and clinicians as the profession developed
- Encourage and facilitate cohorts or students' bonding, and
- Stay organized throughout the semester, especially when assignments are due

COURSE CONSIDERATIONS

Additional Textbooks

The following are suggested textbooks to consider for this course:

- *Orientation to the Counseling Profession: Advocacy, Ethics, and Essential Professional Foundations*, by Bradley T. Erford (2017)

- *Orientation to Professional Counseling*, by Sylvia C. Nassar and Spencer G. Niles (2018)
- *The World of the Counselor: An Introduction to the Counseling Profession*, by Edward S. Neukrug (2015)

Mock Schedule

Exhibit 2.1 is an example of this course's schedule if the chosen book was *The World of the Counselor: An Introduction to the Counseling Profession*, by Edward S. Neukrug (2015).

EXHIBIT 2.1 Orientation to Professional Counseling Courses: Mock Schedule

Class Date	Topics and Readings*
Aug 29th	**Topics:** Introductions; Professor, Peers, Course, Counseling, Ethics **Readings:** Chapter 1: Professional Orientation Chapter 2: The Counseling Profession's Past, Present, and Future
Sep 5th	**Topics:** Introduction to Counseling Process (Calling a Client to Termination); ACA/ASCA Code of Ethics (Principles/Ethical Dilemmas); Accreditation, Licensure, Certifications **Reading:** Chapter 3: Ethics, Accreditation, Credentialing, and the Standards
Sep 12th	**Topic:** Areas of the Counseling Field **Readings:** Chapter 16: School Counseling Chapter 17: Clinical Mental Health Counseling Chapter 18: Student Affairs and College Counseling

(continued)

EXHIBIT 2.1 Orientation to Professional Counseling Courses: Mock Schedule (*continued*)

Class Date	Topics and Readings*
Sep 19th	*Topic:* Theoretical Approaches to Counseling *Reading:* Chapter 4: Individual Approaches to Counseling
Sep 26th	*Topics:* Phases of Counseling; Counseling Skills *Reading:* Chapter 5: Counseling Skills
Oct 3rd	*Topic:* Diagnosis *Reading:* Chapter 10: Abnormal Development, Diagnosis, and Psychopharmacology, pp. 338–341 on Ethical Concerns Regarding Diagnosing
Oct 10th	No Class, Fall Holiday
Oct 17th	*Topic:* Multicultural Counseling *Readings:* Chapter 14: Theory and Concepts of Multicultural Counseling Chapter 15: Knowledge and Skills of Multicultural Counseling
Oct 24th	*Topic:* Working With Families *Reading:* Chapter 6: Couples & Family Counseling, pp. 212–216 on Ethical Concerns Pertaining to Marriage and Family Counseling
Oct 31st	*Topic:* Working With Groups *Reading:* Chapter 7: Group Work

(continued)

EXHIBIT 2.1 Orientation to Professional Counseling Courses: Mock Schedule (*continued*)

Class Date	Topics and Readings*
Nov 7th	*Topic:* Life-Span Approaches *Reading:* Chapter 9: Development Across the Life Span
Nov 14th	*Topic:* Distance Counseling *Reading:* New Concepts in the ACA Code of Ethics, Interview by David Kaplan and Erin Martz
Nov 21st	*Topics:* Supervision; Counselor Education *Reading:* Chapter 8: Consultation and Supervision
Nov 28th	*Topics:* Testing and Assessment; Research and Evaluation *Readings:* Chapter 12: Testing and Assessment Chapter 13: Research and Evaluation
Dec 5th	*Topics:* Finding a Job: Being Interviewed; Applying for Doctoral Programs *Reading:* Afterword, p. 600
Dec 12th	Final Exam

*Listed readings refer to Neukrug, E. (2015). *The world of the counselor: An introduction to the counseling profession* (5th ed.). Boston, MA: Cengage.

ACA, American Counseling Association; ASCA, American School Counselor Association.

COURSE ASSIGNMENTS

Counseling Experience Assignment

The following assignment description was developed by Gerald Pennie, PhD, LPC, NCC. Most students have some experience with counseling. Either through personal or familial experience, students can discuss, even tangentially, the counseling process. To help students process the rapid growth and transformation they are experiencing, I (Gerald) assign a Counseling Experience Assignment. The assignment is simple in terms of what students would need to do to complete it. I ask each student to attend a minimal of six sessions over the course of the semester with proof of attendance and a reflection paper due at the end of the semester.

This assignment is complicated—I do not want to put undue financial distress on students—while counseling has shown to have great benefit. It is important to consider campus-wide resources as they relate to student access to counseling on campus. If your university has the resources, this would be an ideal assignment for the Professional Orientation course.

Annotated Bibliography/Literature Review and Advocacy Project

The following assignment description was developed by Gerald Pennie, PhD, LPC, NCC. Few, if any, students have prior exposure to research. Most have an interest in learning more about a topic or modality that may be related to counseling, and they are overwhelmed by the nature of numbers and statistics. This assignment is vital to helping them develop confidence and competence related to understanding current trends in the counseling profession. This assignment has three parts, each graded individually, and is done over the course of the semester.

The first part, the Annotated Bibliography, requires that each student select a topic of interest. This topic typically centers on some issue in which they are interested and has some form of advocacy attached to it. Students find current literature about the topic and will need at least 10 sources. The students then submit an annotated bibliography, each citation having at least a one-page annotation. This assignment gives students exposure to reputable sources for information, proper APA formatting for a variety of sources, and summarization and citation skills. These skills become extremely valuable throughout the course of the program.

The next part of the assignment is the Literature Review. Students are expected to take their annotated bibliographies, and using a quasi-systematic review, they select research questions to help them select no more than five sources to build a high-quality integrated literature review. This assignment requires that they go beyond summarizing and move toward synthesizing and integrating the findings from the literature into a coherent and concise submission. This assignment is organized as follows: (a) Introduction, (b) Analysis, and (c) Discussion. Within the Introduction section, students discuss the topic they selected using a thesis statement to provide a road map for the paper. This section also includes a segment on inclusion criteria in which the students discuss how they narrowed down their number of sources from the massive number of articles they found initially to the five remaining sources.

The next section of the assignment is Analysis. It centers on the students performing the literature review. Students discuss and integrate their findings from the literature and organize them by themes or research questions. Typically, students focus their writing on themes and integrate the results from their chosen articles. This allows students to try to develop skills that will be beneficial for those who want to continue toward a terminal degree or have a desire to participate in scholarship as well as understanding scholarship.

The next section is the Discussion section. Here the students can critique the current body of literature while providing suggestions for future research. This section includes Limitations, Directions for Future Research, Clinical Impacts/Implications, and Conclusion. This section of the paper is probably one of the most difficult to write. For the first time in writing, students are encouraged to try to combine their entry-level clinical impressions and relevant research to discuss problems, solutions, and implications for the counseling profession.

The final part of this semester-long project is the Advocacy Project. This project is submitted at the end of the semester and combines research and art. Students submit a brochure, newsletter, video, or any other form of media to advocate for the population most affected by the topic about which they chose to write in their literature review. Students are tasked with making an attractive advocacy product that they can give to members of their chosen audience. For instance, one student developed a newsletter with pictures and information, while another student developed a website to advocate for the population chosen. Students use relevant statistics from reputable sources that paint a picture of the problem and give the audience things to do to engage and support this population.

Action Reflection Paper Assignment

The following assignment was developed and discussed by Jude Austin, PhD, LPC, LMFT-Associate, NCC, CCMHC. The following reflection papers are designed to help students critically examine their own values and beliefs.

Action: Interview a Licensed Professional Counselor, LPC-I or Counselor in Residency, Licensed School

Counselor, Licensed Marriage and Family Therapist or LMFT-Associate. The purpose of this interview is to both gather information about their experience as a counselor and inquire about an ethical dilemma they have faced. Questions to ask in the interview include the following:

- What does a typical day look like for you?
- What do you like about your job?
- What do you dislike about your job?
- What is one thing you wish you knew about the field of counseling before you entered (e.g., licensure process, finding a job, salary, residency)?
- Have you ever felt like you made a mistake while counseling from which you learned something?
- Can you name an ethical dilemma that you have been in and explain how you resolved/ handled it?
- Summarize the counselor's responses.

Reflection: What did you learn from this interview that was new or surprising to you? How do you feel about this new information? In terms of the ethical dilemma, how do you feel the counselor handled it? Would you do anything differently?

REFERENCES

Austin, J. T., & Austin, J. A. (2018). Initial exploration of therapeutic presence pedagogy in counselor education. *International Journal for the Advancement of Counselling*, 40(4), 481–500. doi:10.1007/s10447-018-9339-x

Brott, P. E., & Myers, J. E. (1999). Development of professional school counselor identity. *Professional School Counseling*, 2(5), 339–348. Retrieved from https://libres.uncg.edu/ir/uncg/f/j_myers_development_1999.pdf

Duncan, B. L., Miller, S. D., Wampold, B. E., & Hubble, M. A. (2010). *The heart and soul of change: Delivering what works in therapy*. Washington, DC: American Psychological Association.

Erford, B. T. (2017). *Orientation to the counseling profession: Advocacy, ethics, and essential professional foundations*. Columbus, OH: Pearson.

Geller, S. M., & Greenberg, L. S. (2002). Therapeutic presence: Therapists' experience of presence in the psychotherapy encounter. *Person-Centered and Experiential Psychotherapies, 1*(1–2), 71–86. doi:10.1080/14779757.2002.9688279

Geller, S. M., Greenberg, L. S., & Watson, J. G. (2010). Therapist and client perceptions of therapeutic presence: The development of a measure. *Psychotherapy Research, 20*(5), 599–610. doi:10.1080/10503307.2010.495957

Guo, Y. M., Klein, B. D., & Ro, Y. K. (2019). On the effects of student interest, self-efficacy, and perceptions of the instructor on flow, satisfaction, and learning outcomes. *Studies in Higher Education*. doi:10.1080/03075079.2019.1593348

Kaplan, D. M., Tarvydas, V. M., & Gladding, S. T. (2014). 20/20: A vision for the future of counseling: The new consensus definition of counseling. *Journal of Counseling and Development, 92*(3), 366–372. doi:10.1002/j.1556-6676.2014.00164.x

Lee, C. C. (Ed.). (2018). *Counseling for social justice*. Hoboken, NJ: John Wiley & Sons.

Skovholt, T. M., & Ronnestad, M. H. (1992). Themes in therapist and counselor development. *Journal of Counseling and Development, 70*(4), 505–515. doi:10.1002/j.1556-6676.1992.tb01646.x

3 | ETHICS COURSES

INTRODUCTION

Clients are vulnerable. They seek counseling and put their trust in clinicians to provide effective treatment. Without intentionality and adherence to this profession's ethical guidelines, clinicians may harm clients. Ethics courses focus on the codes of ethics for professional counselors, marriage and family therapists, and school counselors. Students will also discuss ethical dilemmas they may face that may not be specifically addressed in an ethical code. When faced with these dilemmas, students will be taught to use an ethical decision-making model.

COURSE DESCRIPTION

Programs should rename Ethics courses "How to Avoid Going to Jail" because most students see "Ethics" and think the worst. Whether or not a clinical decision will be punishable by imprisonment is a topic of fixation for some students. There is always one brave student who asks about the legitimacy of this worry. The class snickers when the question is posed, but everyone is keenly aware of the instructor's answer. At this point, students are introduced to the runner-up for alternate course names, and the bane of counseling students' existence: "It depends." So much of this course centers around helping students grapple ambiguity. There are some ethical situations where the best course of action is straightforward. Other situations require reasoning and involve an uncomfortable level of uncertainty for clinicians. Counselor educators are teaching students how to trust their ability to reason through difficult ethical and moral dilemmas in session. This course has served its purpose if students can leave with confidence in their ethical decision-making and with the humility to seek out support when facing a difficult dilemma.

COURSE OBJECTIVES

The following are course objectives to consider when designing a course on ethics. Upon completion of this course, students will be able to explain the purpose of the Code of Ethics for various associations such as the American Counseling Association (ACA), the American Association for Marriage and Family Therapy (AAMFT), and the American School Counselor Association (ASCA). Students will describe the differences between values, morals, and ethics. Then, students can evaluate their perceptions about professional and ethical issues in counseling and identify personal values, beliefs, and assumptions that may affect ethical practice. Students will be able to recognize the difference between ethical issues and ethical dilemmas. Using an ethical decision-making model, students will be able to resolve ethical dilemmas and issues. They will also be able to understand the ethical issues involved in assessment, training, and supervision. Finally, students will apply ethical standards to case examples, simulations, and role-plays.

MUST-COVER TOPICS

Ethical practice in the counseling profession is constantly changing and evolving as counselors face an increasingly complex world. The following is a brief discussion about important topics covered in this course.

Technology

As technological advances increase, so do the methods to deliver counseling services. Counselors are accessible to clients more now than in the last decade. Clients can reach their clinicians via text, phone calls, email, social media, and other forms of e-communications. These types of communications present potential issues of privacy, confidentiality, methods of encryption, clients' access to treatment records, and informed consent. They increase the need to address the vulnerability of emails, phones, or computer communications when a client begins treatment (Goss, Anthony, Stretch, & Nagel, 2016). Technology's impact on the work counselors do and the communities they serve is an important topic to cover in this course.

In addition to technology being a source of communicating with and providing services for clients, it can also be used to obtain information about therapists. Students must be more intentional about how they present themselves to their clients in person and online. Clients can google their therapists, friend request them on social media, or review social pages and listservs. Clients are curious, which is a natural part of any relationship. It may be helpful for students to occasionally goggle themselves and visit their social media pages as a guest to see what clients might be able to discover about them.

Health Insurance Portability and Accountability Act

The Health Insurance Portability and Accountability Act (HIPAA) is an essential piece of a counselor's education. It is designed to protect clients from losing their health insurance if they change residences, jobs, or health plans.

It also provides increased protection against fraud. It covers client confidentiality, electronic storage and transmission, and clients' rights regarding autonomy, privacy, and accessibility to records. HIPAA is the standard of care for counselors today. Even if clinicians do not submit electronic billing, they still must be HIPAA compliant. This is due to the new additions that cover more than billing. Students should be particularly aware of Psychotherapy Notes, Minimum Necessary, and Need to Know.

Confidentiality

This topic is constantly evolving and changing as the profession goes. Each state has its own laws and regulations regarding confidentiality. Additionally, each professional association has its own standards regarding how to practice confidentiality. Then, each clinic and workplace have their own specific nuances regarding keeping client information confidential. Today's students are facing a professional world with evolving complexities regarding this topic. Counselor educators need to constantly grow in their understanding of confidentiality each year.

Record Keeping

How clinicians keep records, like confidentiality, is ever evolving. Private practitioners have digital platform options such as TherapyAppointment.com and TherapyNotes.com. These platforms allow a clinician to schedule clients, send documents, maintain charts or notes, bill insurance, and communicate with clients. Students may also use the Titanium platform or pen and paper. Whichever option they choose or are trained to use when maintaining client records, students need to be taught how to maintain them ethically.

Dual Relationships

This topic is somewhat controversial in that official stances change subtly with each revision of ethical standards. It is a topic in which discussion and reason will serve students best. Past practitioners thought dual relationships lead to harm, either through exploitation or inappropriate sexual relationships. Now, many clinicians and ethics committees understand how difficult it is for therapists in small communities to avoid dual relationships. Many circumstances influence how clinicians navigate dual relationships with clients. Students need to understand where their association, state, and community stand on this topic.

Therapeutic Boundaries

There has been a shift in the profession toward a more flexible and context-based application of therapeutic boundaries. If there was ever a case to reiterate the phrase "It depends," it would be when discussing this topic. Within the discussion of therapeutic boundaries, counselor educators may also focus on subtopics such as self-disclosure, bartering, therapeutic touch, experiences out of the office, and adventure therapy.

Subpoenas

Getting records subpoenaed is perhaps one of the most fear-charged topics for students. Again, some students worry about being arrested, losing their licenses, or harming their clients. Responding to a subpoena is complicated because of the conflicts between ethical standards and state legal requirements. Therapists must consider a host of factors when deciding how to respond to a subpoena.

Discussing these factors can lower anxiety and help students feel less helpless.

Ethical Decision-Making Model

As discussed earlier, counselors face an increasingly complex world. Each case and clinical situation is contextually different. Cases can present challenges that are difficult to navigate when clinicians are juggling a full caseload. An ethical decision-making model lays out steps for counselors to follow when faced with an ethical issue or dilemma. Forester-Miller and Davis's (1995) model is particularly helpful with students because of its comprehensive and easy-to-follow guidelines. This model focuses on five foundational principles: autonomy, justice, beneficence, nonmaleficence, and fidelity. The model also organizes steps for counselors to follow when faced with an ethical issue:

1. Identify the problem.
2. Apply the ACA Code of Ethics.
3. Determine the nature and dimensions of the dilemma.
4. Generate potential courses of action.
5. Consider the potential consequences of all options and determine a course of action.
6. Evaluate the selected course of action.
7. Implement the course of action.

PERSONAL EXPERIENCE

The following sections involve a brief discussion of our experience teaching this course. As in the previous chapter, we focus our discussion on our teaching approach, student experiences, course preparation, the nuts and bolts of the course, and our advice for counselor educators.

Teaching Approach

We have taught and experienced ethics courses as students in one of two ways: at a distance and relationally. One form of this course is dominated by class presentations. Counselor educators split the students into small groups and assign a different ethical code to each group. Each group gets assigned a day to lead the class in an examination and discussion of a section of the ethical code. As counselor educators using this approach, we found it to be easier to prep for the course but more difficult to manage the student learning. Group leadership can be unpredictable. Some groups are more prepared and organized than others. Students' class experience is heavily dependent on the groups' ability to lead the discussion. Another form of this course is lecture and clinically balanced. The first part of the class is focused on the ethical standards, and another part of the class is dedicated to presenting and discussing a clinical vignette. The vignette is practical and complex, presenting multiple contextual elements for students to consider when making an ethical decision.

Much like Professional Orientation courses, this course needs space to breathe. Students need room to grapple with the gray areas of ethics. The answers are not always black or white, right or wrong. There are many contextual factors involved with facing ethical issues and dilemmas. Given this need, we approach teaching this course using a Socratic method. This approach requires active engagement from both the students and the counselor educator. It is driven by questions, which allows students to think through their actions and perspective. Students must ask themselves why they do the things they do and think the way they do.

This Socratic method is less about hearing the correct answers in certain discussions and more about pushing students to be creative when approaching a problem. When processing the material in this way, students are able to connect the lecture information with the contextual issues involved in their cases. This discussion-based learning trains the person of the therapist. Students help others as they talk through a specific case. Counselor educators are humble enough to say "I do not know." That phrase humanizes the counselor educator and models for students the reasoning process. Facilitating the students' process of slowly walking through an ethical decision-making model for every ethical issue and dilemma builds strong professional habits.

Student Experience

When approaching the course using groups and the presenters and discussion leaders, feedback was polarizing. Some students appreciated the chance to present and to take more responsibility for their learning. Other feedback focused on the inconsistency from class to class. When counselor educators take the primary role in leading discussions, classes tend to fall into a rhythm. Students find comfort in that rhythm. As counselor educators leading the course in this way, it seemed as though the course struggled to find its rhythm because each class felt like starting over in some ways. However, the students struggled with their ethical decision model and seemed to rely on each other to reason through problems. This modeled the consultation style and professional communication that may serve them as they begin practicing independently.

Feedback surrounding the more balanced, counselor educator–led approach highlighted the practical nature of the course as a strength. Other students shared their frustration with the ambiguity of the class. This ambiguity creates dialogue that allows students who may not verbally participate for unknown reasons to take something away from the discussions. This approach can, however, lead students down a frustration spiral that leaves them exhausted by the end of class and needing to know what the instructor would do. This is how most of the classes ended when using this approach.

Course Preparation

We enjoy teaching the course using the second, more Socratic approach. We find it to be more challenging and stimulating for students. To facilitate an experience that feels fluid and discussion oriented takes detailed planning and intentionality on class day. However, sometimes a case or a specific topic in a case triggers an unexpected discussion, which then feels unproductive. The challenge in this course is to spin the discussions, no matter how far off track they seem, into something useful for the class. Students are often surprised when we share our daily class outlines at how organized the class is, despite its free-flowing feeling. There is quite a bit of intentionality regarding the plan.

The heavy lifting regarding weekly prepping for this course is done before the semester starts. Organizing each class's vignettes and process questions before the semester clears space during the week. This space allows for time to familiarize ourselves with the current literature surrounding the ethical standard or topic of the class. If our class is scheduled for Thursday, we might start preparing on Tuesday. The state laws and ethical standards from various organizations offer the content we will present to students. Oftentimes when creating a presentation, our focus is on breaking down the language used in the standards. The lecture supports the discussion and provides students with the knowledge they need to process the case.

In each class, we prepare a brief PowerPoint lecture focused on the ethical standard or law chosen for that class period. We also prepare a case vignette with a summary of the client background and relevant information about the case. These cases are from a variety of disciplines: school counseling, marriage and family therapy, and clinical mental health. Along with the case, we prepare about 5 to 10 process questions to put students in the position of the clinician. We want them to internalize the experience and discuss it as if they are experiencing it in the moment. Along with the questions, we provide an ethical decision-making model for each case. We found that students respond well to Forester-Miller and Davis's (1995) ethical decision-making model. They have revised this model in 2016, which can be found on the ACA website.

The challenge of preparing for this course is letting go of control. There is an element of approaching the course in this way that is unknown. This course is affected by class culture and students' energy levels. Preparing for this course encourages us to trust the process, and it is hard to do so with so many contextual factors to be mindful of during discussions. We address these challenges by organizing the class process. Having a class outline for each day helps us to feel in control of the process. We may not be able to control what each student will say, but we can control the flow of the discussion and the timing. This provides a small amount of comfort.

Nuts and Bolts

As discussed earlier, this class's discussions can be free flowing and lead the class down unintended rabbit holes. Managing these discussions is key to staying on track in class. It may be beneficial to identify two to five key points students can take away from each class and focus on identifying those points when discussed in class.

Sometimes, depending on the topic, we open the class with time for questions. For example, on the day we are discussing ways to respond to a subpoena, we may open the class with time for questions. Getting those initial questions addressed can settle the class into the lecture and help them process the case vignette.

Due to a class's potential propensity to be sidetracked during discussions, we address this with the class during the first meeting. We share with them our experience and discuss ways, such as signals, to bring their attention back to the topic. After the discussions and attempts to pull the class back on topic, this process becomes part of the course culture, and students are usually able to focus themselves.

Grading assignments and papers feels less overwhelming in this course than in other courses, perhaps because the assignments and papers involve following students' logic as opposed to their correctness. However, we experience the assignments and papers as being due relatively close together. Therefore, it is important for counselor educators to attack each assignment once turned in to avoid being overwhelmed. In addition, some assignments can be graded in real time. For example, class presentations can be graded when students are presenting, by following the presentation rubric. We discuss some potential assignments here.

We do not often give quizzes in a course. As students, we often studied to pass the quiz and not to integrate the information into our professional identity. However, as counselor educators, we understand that this course covers the content, but much of the learning occurs during discussions. Therefore, we use the course's online platform to conduct daily quizzes regarding the various associations' Codes of Ethics. In addition to the quizzes, students will have full access to the case vignettes with our breakdown of the case and a discussion of the ethical decision-making model. Students will have access to these resources after each class period.

Advice

Ethics courses are challenging and exciting to teach. It is a creative and process-oriented experience. We enjoy the unpredictability of the discussions. It is also humbling processing a case where there are multiple correct choices and a student chooses a course of action different and more correct than ours at times. We also enjoy watching students grow processing ethical issues and dilemmas with confidence. Some of our favorite moments in class are when students get lost in a discussion about the best way to care for a client. As counselor educators we can sit and listen to this discussion for 5 minutes before the class gets stuck and looks for guidance. We may share one or two sentences, and then the class picks up the discussion again. As students' confidence grows and they learn to take themselves through the ethical decision-making model, the longer they can discuss without looking for guidance.

A pitfall to be aware of when teaching an ethics course is the constantly evolving professional landscape, rules, and regulations. Students will have questions, and counselor educators are not expected to answer all these questions. However, not knowing some answers can cause confusion in class. Another pitfall to be aware of is imposing our values upon students. It is important for students to process ethical issues in a safe space where they can share their ideas and potential courses of action, even if these ideas and courses of action differ from the instructor. Another pitfall is giving students too much freedom in discussion. We have experienced students who may tend to dominate discussions and take space away from others who are less outspoken. Counselor educators can help give all students a voice when watching class discussions intently and stepping in to support less talkative students.

Tips to be successful when teaching an Ethics course are as follows:

- Give students space to process their thoughts, feelings, and actions.
- Trust the process, which to us means that learning is happening even when students are stuck.
- Monitor discussions so that they are productive.
- Counselor educators should consider their biases when faced with ethical issues and dilemmas.
- Find the balance for the class between unproductive frustration and productive frustration. This is particularly important when students are faced with gray areas and the phrase "It depends."
- Openly discuss anxiety around making ethical decisions. This normalizes their experience.

COURSE CONSIDERATIONS

This section briefly covers course considerations such as textbooks and course schedule. As always, these are suggestions that can be used as a starting point.

Additional Textbooks

Some textbooks to consider when teaching this course are:

- *Issues and Ethics in the Helping Professions*, by Gerald Corey, Marianne S. Corey, and Patrick Callanan (2014)
- *Ethical, Legal, and Professional Issues in Counseling*, by Theodore (Ted) Remley and Barbara Herlihy (2014)
- *Ethics in Psychotherapy and Counseling: A Practical Guide*, by Kenneth S. Pope (2016)

- *Ethics in Counseling & Psychotherapy*, by Elizabeth Reynolds Welfel (2015)
- *School Counseling Principles: Ethics + Law*, by Carolyn Stone, EdD (2006)
- *Ethical, Legal, and Professional Issues in the Practice of Marriage and Family Therapy*, by Allen P. Wilcoxon, Remley Jr., P. Theodore, and Samuel T. Gladding (2013)

Mock Schedule

A potential course schedule may look like the example in Exhibit 3.1.

EXHIBIT 3.1 Ethics Course: Mock Schedule

Class Date	Topics and Readings*
Jan 16	*Topics:* Introductions; Professor, Peers, Course, Counseling, Ethics
Jan 23	*Topics:* Introduction to Counseling Process (Calling a Client to Termination); ACA/ASCA Code of Ethics (Principles/Ethical Dilemmas); Accreditation, Licensure, Certifications *Readings:* Ethics, Accreditation, Credentialing, and the Standards
Jan 30	*Readings:* *A Practitioner's Guide to Ethical Decision Making* ACA Section I: Resolving Ethical Issues
Feb 6	*Reading:* ACA Section B: Confidentiality and Privacy
Feb 13	*Reading:* ACA Section A: The Counseling Relationship

(continued)

EXHIBIT 3.1 Ethics Course: Mock Schedule (*continued*)

Class Date	Topics and Readings*
Feb 20	*Reading:* ACA Section C: Professional Responsibility
Feb 27	*Readings:* Chapter 14: Theory and Concepts of Multicultural Counseling Chapter 15: Knowledge and Skills of Multicultural Counseling
Mar 6	*Topic:* Working With Families *Readings:* Chapter 6: Couples & Family Counseling, pp. 212–216 on Ethical Concerns Pertaining to Marriage and Family Counseling ACA Section D: Relationships With Other Professionals
Mar 13	No Class, Spring Break
Mar 20	*Topic:* Working With Groups *Readings:* ACA Section A: The Counseling Relationship ACA Section B: Confidentiality and Privacy
Mar 27	*Readings:* New Concepts in the ACA Code of Ethics, Interview by David Kaplan and Erin Martz ACA Section H: Distance Counseling, Technology, and Social Media
Apr 3	*Reading:* ACA Section F: Supervision, Training, and Teaching
Apr 10	*Reading:* ACA Section E: Evaluation, Assessment, and Interpretation

(*continued*)

EXHIBIT 3.1 Ethics Course: Mock Schedule
(*continued*)

Class Date	Topics and Readings*
Apr 17	*Reading:* ACA Section G: Research and Publication
Apr 24	*Topic:* Practicing Ethically *Reading:* Afterword, p. 600
May 1	Final Exam

*Listed readings refer to the American Counseling Association. (2014). *2014 code of ethics*. Alexandria, VA: Author; Forester-Miller, H., & Davis, T. E. (1995). *A practitioner's guide to ethical decision making*. Alexandria, VA: American Counseling Association; and Neukrug, E. (2015). *The world of the counselor: An introduction to the counseling profession* (5th ed.). Boston, MA: Cengage.

ACA, American Counseling Association; ASCA, American School Counselor Association.

COURSE ASSIGNMENTS

Article Review

In this assignment, students will provide a written review of at least four professional peer-reviewed journal articles that address ethical issues in clinical mental health counseling, marriage and family therapy, and school counseling. Each written review must be written according to *APA Publication Manual*'s guidelines and no less than two pages in length. Students will summarize the article's literature review, research methods and design, results, and implications to ethical practice.

Ethics Hearing and Reflection Paper

Students will attend an ethical hearing by the state board regarding licensure. Students will then provide a written review of their experiences. In this review, students will outline the cases they witnessed and the applicable ethical codes for those cases.

Informed Consent

Students will prepare an informed consent document that addresses all necessary considerations, depending upon each student's concentration area: Clinical Mental Health Counseling, Marriage, Family, Child Counseling, or School Counseling.

Ethical Summary

Students will summarize, in their own words, their understanding of each of the nine sections of the ACA *Code of Ethics*. Students will describe relationships between the *Code of Ethics* sections and the ethical principles. Students will include in this summary an introductory paragraph, a summary paragraph for each section, and a concluding paragraph.

REFERENCES

Forester-Miller, H., & Davis, T. E. (1995). *A practitioner's guide to ethical decision making*. Alexandria, VA: American Counseling Association.

Goss, S., Anthony, K., Stretch, L. S., & Nagel, D. M. (2016). *Technology in mental health: Applications in practice, supervision and training*. Springfield, IL: Charles C. Thomas Publisher.

COUNSELING THEORIES COURSES

INTRODUCTION

The Counseling Theories course could be considered the lifeblood of a counseling program. It sets the tone for master's degree students' experience in not only the counseling program but the way the students conceptualize theory and how students relate theory to practice. This course introduces students, some for the very first time, to the theories designed to guide the practices of counselors. This course also aids students in discovering and building a framework for the process of understanding, interpreting, and putting theory into action. We call this course the "Road Map course" for three reasons. The first reason is because counseling theories can act as maps for beginning counselors, which provide direction when working with clients. The second reason is because, as the students become more settled into internship and the start of their careers, theories help to facilitate the integration process of the skills, philosophy, and self into sessions. Lastly, the third reason is because action in session needs to be immediate. Theory can be instrumental in guiding action or a response to the unpredictable circumstances of therapy.

COURSE DESCRIPTION

This is a foundational course that helps students become acquainted with the philosophical underpinnings of the theoretical orientations used by clinicians to help clients. The most common theories covered in this course tend to be the following:

1. Psychoanalysis
2. Jungian Analysis and Therapy
3. Adlerian Therapy
4. Existential Therapy
5. Person-Centered Therapy
6. Gestalt Therapy
7. Behavior Therapy
8. Rational Emotive Behavior Therapy
9. Cognitive Therapy
10. Reality Therapy
11. Constructivist Approaches
12. Feminist Therapy
13. Family Therapy

These theories serve the purpose of providing a broad basis for a student's orientation into theoretical orientations. It is important to note the difficulty in covering every detail about each theory in a single semester. This course is a brief visit to the edge of the deep caverns that these theories have carved out in the counseling field over time.

Completion of this course will result in the ability to answer the following questions for each theory:

1. What is the history or background of a theory?
2. How does the theory view the nature of personality?
3. How does the theory conceptualize psychological disorders?
4. What are the various approaches to treatment?
5. What are the current trends regarding the theory?
6. How can a specific theory be used with other theories?
7. What is the current research on the theory?

8. How does the theory relate to contemporary multicultural issues?
9. How is the theory used in group therapy?
10. What are suggested readings related to this theory?

Students' ability to answer these questions for each theory can shed light on which theory may best fit their personhood as they matriculate through the counseling program. That light can create a pathway for thoughtful, consistent, responsible, and intentional usage of these theories in session. The course is exploratory in nature, giving students the opportunity to examine the theories for personal congruence and applicability to the populations they will be serving.

This can be a fast-paced course because you are essentially balancing two things: content and experiential learning. The content of these theories has been documented throughout time by the pillars of our field, for example, Gerald Corey, but helping students to understand how these theories function with today's clients needs time, energy, and creativity. As Professor Snape said in *Harry Potter and the Chamber of Secrets*, "you are here to learn the subtle science and exact art of potion-making." This course is a balance between the content of theory and its application and how the theory looks when applied to real/mock situations.

COURSE OBJECTIVES

The course has standard objectives that are usually non-removable from the course syllabi attached to the course in most Council for Accreditation of Counseling and Related Educational Programs (CACREP)-accredited programs. For example, the CACREP standards this course will most likely meet are:

1. Strategies for personal and professional self-evaluation and implications for practice ([f.1.k] 2)
2. Theories and models of counseling ([f.5.a] 3)
3. Ethical and culturally relevant strategies for establishing and maintaining in-person and technology-assisted relationships ([f.5.d] 4)
4. Counselor characteristics and behavior that influence the counseling process ([f.5.f] 5)
5. Essential interviewing, counseling, and case conceptualization skills ([f.5.g] 6)
6. Processes for aiding students in developing a personal model of counseling ([f.5.n] 7)
7. Methods of effectively preparing for and conducting initial assessment meetings ([f.7.b] 8)
8. Theories and models related to clinical mental health counseling ([CMHC c.1.b] 9)
9. Cultural factors relevant to clinical mental health counseling (CMHC c.2.j)

In addition to these course objectives, students will learn characteristics about particular theories and be given the chance to juxtapose them to the time and place of their origin as well as their metamorphoses to contemporary counseling practices. Students should also be given the opportunity to integrate their own life histories and cultures when critically examining the theories. Other course objectives could include the following:

1. Identify major theorists and the therapy they champion.
2. Define terms associated with theories and demonstrate understanding of the terms.
3. Understand and describe the key concepts associated with each theory.
4. List and examine the limitations of each major theory.

5. Explain the therapeutic process of change as expressed by each major theory.
6. Explain the view of human nature expressed by each theory.
7. Identify and describe the therapeutic methods and techniques utilized by each major theory.
8. Understand the therapeutic goals of each theory.
9. Define the therapist's function and role.
10. Understand the client's experience in therapy.
11. Understand and describe the relationship between therapist and client.
12. Compare and contrast theories.
13. Apply each theory to a case study or mock session.
14. Describe the differences between eclecticism and integration of counseling theories.
15. Understand the role of assessment in each theory.
16. Understand how theories can be applied to addiction counseling.
17. Understand how theories can be applied to group counseling.

MUST-COVER TOPICS

Each theory has specific topics that must be covered. This list of "must covers" is not meant to be the end all and be all of topics you should cover in the theories course. It is meant to act as a flexible guide that allows for adaptation depending on your particular class makeup. By using the previously mentioned list of the most common theories covered in this course, you can organize the must-cover topics of each theory in the following way:

Topic 1: Theorists' biography and influences
Topic 2: Key concepts
Topic 3: View of human nature

Topic 4: The therapeutic process
Topic 5: What causes problems for clients?
Topic 6: Role of the client and counselor
Topic 7: Goals of therapy
Topic 8: Application of therapeutic techniques and procedures
Topic 9: Multicultural considerations
Topic 10: Theory applied to mock client/case study

This topic structure can be adapted to your particular course and will add clarity when organizing the consumption of theoretical information. The structure also allows for predictability within the course and the opportunity to cover two or three topics at a time throughout the semester.

Watts (1993) explained that an important question for students who are new to the study of counseling theories pertains to wanting to know how to choose a theory that best fits their personhood. This topic may not be covered in every theorys course, but it is important to note that this question can be saturated with anxiety and confusion for students. For most, this course is the first time they may be hearing that these theories exist. This may cause students to feel the pressure of needing to consume the knowledge and concepts, integrate them into their budding approach to counseling, and use the theories effectively with clients. Covering or at least validating the students' experiences who may be feeling these things is an important part of this course.

PERSONAL EXPERIENCE

The following sections focus on our experience teaching the Counseling Theories courses. Again, our discussions are *a* way to teach these courses, not *the* way to teach them. Our hope is that readers use our experience to better prepare their courses.

Teaching Approach

When approaching this course, we strongly consider the class size, the anxiety level of the class as a whole, and being intentional about using various methods of delivering information to students. This course can be a content-heavy course that can be a gift or a curse. The course can be a curse if students are not made aware of their responsibility to read the course materials before every class, which is key in a class such as this one. We have found that a combination of having a brief PowerPoint, which highlights the specific topics from the theory that will be covered on the day, as well as keeping lecture time short helps students to connect with the material. One of the most important requests from students is "It would really help if I could see the theories being done." Here is where a content-heavy theories course can become experiential, because the theories can come to life for students once they leave the comfort of their required texts and enter the realm of videos/discussions or live mock demonstrations.

In our approach to teaching this course, we are firm believers in the transparent counseling pedagogy (TCP) strategy. Dollarhide, Smith, and Lemberger (2007) explained the TCP process to be a "counselor" and "client" interacting with students to create transparency in the therapeutic process. Operationally, the students start in small groups and watch the counselor and client demonstrate a counseling interaction. Throughout any point in the therapeutic interaction, the counselor can stop the process to ask students to discuss in their small groups questions such as "What would you say next?" or "What did you notice within the interaction?" Then students are asked to express their clinical ideas, rationale, and congruency with the theory being taught that day. It is important that students express their ideas aloud and have agency in choosing the clinical direction in the therapeutic interaction.

When using videos as demonstrations, for example, the Gloria series, we take a similar small-groups approach, breaking the class down into several small sections and giving them specific assignments. One group may be commenting on the relationship between the client and counselor. Another group may be looking for any key concepts that may come out of the video. The issue that we found with videos or any type of demonstration of a theory in practice is that students may get the idea that the example portrayed in the video is the "right" way to practice a particular theory. It is important to discuss subtle nuances that may shift the demonstration of a theory depending on the clinician who is demonstrating.

Student Experience

From the beginning of the course, students experience us as knowing a little about the theories covered in the course, but we make it clear that we are not experts on any theory. We are also genuine about the particular theoretical orientation that we use as clinicians and how the development of our clinical work from a theoretical perspective is ever growing and evolving the training and experience we acquire. Our goal is for students to see us as people who can speak about what it is really like to use a technique from any theory in practice. We want our students to experience us as a voice from the field who can not only teach the information but personalize the experience of a beginning counselor learning the information for the first time and feeling the pressure to consume and use it in the future.

With regard to making it known to students what theoretical orientation we use as clinicians, we also want our students to know that any demonstration done by us in class will have our style embedded into it, which means that whatever theory is being demonstrated will have our way of being with clients in the fabric of the therapeutic interactions. We want to make this clear because we have found it hard to bracket out our own way of being during demonstrations. Mentioning to students that, at times, they might get a mixture of the theory we are covering for the day as well as a hint of our way of doing things in session humanizes us and normalizes the fact that clinical demonstrations are rarely perfect.

It is also important to mention to students that this course will force some to look within themselves to really try to understand how they view human nature or how others develop issues or maladaptive behaviors. The awareness of these notions may change the way students view themselves or the way they interact with those closest to them. We especially see a shift with students during the middle of the semester or when they find a theoretical orientation with which they connect and that helps them to put life circumstances into perspective. Also, students may feel the urge to practice what they learned from specific theories on their significant others or friends and family members. We just make students aware of those urges and the possible drawbacks from giving in to them.

Course Preparation

Preparation for a theories course starts the second you hear that you will be teaching this course because it will take a considerable amount of time to reacquaint yourself with the theories being covered. Because there is an abundance of resources available, some theories have their own library of information; take time to narrow down materials to be used in the course. If multiple online books, journal articles, and videos are planned to be used, then time should be allocated to find the appropriate ones with working links. Here, we briefly share our experience preparing for this course.

If the course is scheduled for Wednesdays from 5:00 p.m. to 7:50 p.m. and today is Monday, we would start preparing for this course on the Thursday of the previous week. We would start by examining the book chapter and keeping in the back of our heads which topics will be covered for the class period. We would break the class into three time slots: (a) introduction and PowerPoint lecture, (b) experiential activity (demonstration, video, etc.), and (c) questions, concerns, and assignment check-ins. Each time slot takes 1 to 3 hours to prepare for depending on the content being presented.

The first time slot, introduction and PowerPoint lecture, takes the longest because we usually make 30 to 50 slides for an initial draft and pare that down to 15 to 20 slides for the final lecture. We like to read the chapters and make notes in the margins on what we would like to cover and organize our lecture based on what would make sense for our students. It is also important to keep in mind that there needs to be flex time built into the lecture based on a specific focus to which students may be drawn. For example, one class might be more prone to specific questions about the therapeutic relationship and the ins and outs of the role of the counselor. So, the lecture can give more time to those areas, answering a lot of student questions before they have a chance to form.

The second time slot, experiential activity, is the most unpredictable and tedious. If the activity involves a guest speaker, then this guest speaker needs to be contacted months before the scheduled time to speak to make arrangements. If the activity is a video, then the video needs to be watched in its entirety to ensure that it is appropriate for the particular lesson, but specific minute marks need to be made so that teachable moments can be designed to fit into the video. If the activity is a mock therapeutic interaction, then thought and compassion need to go into planning the specific direction that this interaction needs to take to get what is needed to cover the theory at hand.

The third time slot, questions, concerns, and assignment check-ins, may seem simple and pressure free, but this time is one of the most important in class. Checking in with students regarding questions they have about what was covered in the course and what will be covered in the future can ease anxiety of students who like to begin assignments early. It can also provide a quick summary of information that was covered for students who may have missed a particular topic or piece of information during the course. Checking in with students about assignments also can ease tension of the students who start assignments early, but it also gives you an opportunity to gain insight into what students find the most confusing so that it can be changed for future classes.

Nuts and Bolts

On class day, how do you manage time and stay on track? Like most courses, managing time and staying on track in class is a matter of creating a conscious blueprint to create direction in this course. In this course it is easy to get bogged down in the lecture points and have that time bleed into the experiential portion of the class. There has to be a certain strictness with regard to managing time in class in order to move from lecture to demonstration in this course because we treat them as equally important. We create natural breaks in class to transition from one topic to the next or from one method of portraying information to the next. For example, if the class goes from 5:00 p.m. to 7:50 p.m., then introduction and lecture will start at 5:00 p.m. and end at 6:00 p.m. with a 15-minute break at the end. The experiential activity will start at 6:15 p.m. and end at 7:25 p.m. Lastly, checking in with students about assignments, questions, or concerns will begin at 7:25 p.m. and end at 7:50 p.m.

An additional element to this course is managing assignments. Regardless of how many assignments exist in the course, strictness of time needs to be applied here as well. Also, we found that this course was easier to manage when we took the course size into account and decided on what type of grading was realistic for us. We have had colleagues in the past who decided to load the course assignments, making the time to grade these assignments enter the realm of a 4-week wait for students.

For us, creating assignments that are a mixture of understanding the content and application while also challenging the students and promoting self-exploration and growth does not equate to a 4-week wait period. For us, reading papers and providing feedback needs to be done in a quick yet impactful manner. So, a combination of quizzes and short consistent papers allows us to help students develop as writers and also gives in-depth feedback in a timely manner. We also use online course resources (Canvas, Blackboard, Moodle, etc.) to help students stay on top of their grades. This course is usually taken at the beginning of the journey for master's degree students. Creating assignments that challenge thinking and promote self-exploration is pivotal for students at this stage in their education. Also, allowing for transparency and awareness of where they stand in the course can limit anxious feelings and confusion.

Advice

This course is usually grouped in the course sequence at the beginning of a student's time in the program. It is usually the first time that students have encountered these theories. It could also be a student's first introduction into graduate school–level expectations. There will be a combination of anxiety-producing factors that are at play in this course. These are all of our favorite components of teaching this course. We realized that because this is usually the first graduate-level course, holding students' anxiety about the theories are sometimes very simple compared to holding their anxiety about graduate-level expectations. Students usually come into this class with perfectionistic tendencies, which can cause issues when "needing to get things right" in a demonstration (Jiao & Onwuegbuzie, 1998). Students often put too much pressure on themselves to learn every facet of every theory or even to make a certain grade no matter how much information is actually learned.

One of the biggest revelations we have had when teaching this course is that the counseling theories course is pivotal to students' careers. Knowing these theories and understanding how to use them in session or how they fit within their personhood are deeply important. But what may be more important is that students have the type of experience in this course that sparks continued learning and exploration of theory and practice for the rest of their careers. If we were teaching this course for the first time, we would have done the following:

1. Made sure we knew the theories inside and out or until we felt comfortable to teach them
2. Gone outside the textbook and incorporated journal articles into the lectures
3. Booked guest speakers who currently use the specific theory of the day currently in practice
4. Spent less time preparing lectures of things we think are important for students to know and listened more to students' needs
5. Created specific times and days for class prep time and grading time—and keep it!
6. Not put so much pressure on ourselves to perform well during any therapeutic demonstrations

COURSE CONSIDERATIONS

Additional Textbooks

The following is a list of suggested textbooks counselor educators can consider when preparing for this course:

- *Theory and Practice of Counseling and Psychotherapy* (10th ed.), by Gerald Corey (2016)
- *Counseling and Psychotherapy: Theories and Interventions*, by David Capuzzi and Mark D. Stauffer (2016)
- *Counseling Theory and Practice*, by Edward Neukrug (2017)
- *Theories and Applications of Counseling and Psychotherapy: Relevance Across Cultures and Settings*, by Earl J. Ginter, Gargi Roysircar, and Lawrence H. Gerstein (2018)

Mock Schedule

The mock schedule in Exhibit 4.1 is constructed as if the course textbook is *Theory and Practice of Counseling and Psychotherapy* (10th ed.), by Gerald Corey (2016).

EXHIBIT 4.1 Counseling Theories: Mock Schedule

Week	Description
1	Review syllabus and class requirements Read Chapters 1 and 2 in the textbook* Complete the Introduction Form
2	Read Chapters 3 and 4
3	Read Chapter 5 View videos on Moodle and complete the Video Reaction Form for the video indicated Complete the case study
4	Read Chapter 6 View videos on Moodle and complete the Video Reaction Form for the video indicated Complete the case study

(continued)

EXHIBIT 4.1 Counseling Theories: Mock Schedule (*continued*)

Week	Description
5	Read Chapter 7 View videos on Moodle and complete the Video Reaction Form for the video indicated Complete the case study
6	Read Chapter 8 View videos on Moodle and complete the Video Reaction Form for the video indicated Complete the case study
7	Midterm
8	Read Chapter 9 View videos on Moodle and complete the Video Reaction Form for the video indicated Complete the case study
9	Read Chapter 10 View videos on Moodle and complete the Video Reaction Form for the video indicated Complete the case study
10	Read Chapter 11 View videos on Moodle and complete the Video Reaction Form for the video indicated Complete the case study
11	Read Chapter 12 View videos on Moodle and complete the Video Reaction Form for the video indicated Complete the case study
12	Read Chapter 13 View videos on Moodle and complete the Video Reaction Form for the video indicated Complete the case study
13	Read Chapter 14 View videos on Moodle and complete the Video Reaction Form for the video indicated Complete the case study

(*continued*)

EXHIBIT 4.1 Counseling Theories: Mock Schedule (*continued*)

Week	Description
14	Read Chapter 15 View videos on Moodle and complete the Video Reaction Form for the video indicated Complete the case study
15	Final Exam

*Listed reading refers to Corey, G. (2016). *Theory and practice of counseling and psychotherapy* (10th ed.). Boston, MA: Cengage Learning.

COURSE ASSIGNMENTS

Theory Comparison Paper

Students will choose three theories to compare. Students are to critically examine how these theories are alike and how they differ. Students will discuss the following: personality formation or view of human nature, how change occurs, key concepts, the therapeutic process, counselor's role, and so forth. All theory discussion should begin with an introduction to each theory before the comparisons and contrasting begin. The paper is to be seven to eight pages and double spaced using a font of 12. There should be a minimum of six references. References should be no older than 5 years and can be a combination of books and journal articles. The paper must be done in American Psychological Association (APA) format.

Weekly Journal

Throughout this course, students are to keep a weekly journal. Once a week, students will document their experiences as they pertain to the class and the theory. Students are to describe the material they are reading, their conceptualizations of the theory, the portions of the theory that make sense, the parts they wonder about, and their perceived congruence and dissonance with the theory or theories based on their observations, life experience, and interactions with classmates. Each journal entry should be at least half a typed page.

Preliminary Theoretical "Leanings" Paper

On the third week of class, students will submit a two-page paper reflecting on any preliminary theoretical leanings. In this paper, student will propose a personal theory (based only on material already acquired and on personal observations/theories) as to what causes suffering and what helps people change. There are no references required. This is a chance for students to begin exploring what their personal beliefs about counseling and psychotherapy are, in hopes that, as the semester ensues, students' beliefs can begin to blend and integrate with theories studied in class. The paper should be typed and double spaced and follow APA format.

REFERENCES

Dollarhide, C. T., Smith, A. T., & Lemberger, M. E. (2007). Counseling made transparent: Pedagogy for a counseling theories course. *Counselor Education and Supervision, 46*(4), 242–253. doi:10.1002/j.1556-6978.2007.tb00029.x

Jiao, Q. G., & Onwuegbuzie, A. J. (1998). Perfectionism and library anxiety among graduate students. *The Journal of Academic Librarianship, 24*(5), 365–371. doi:10.1016/S0099-1333(98)90073-8

Watts, R. E. (1993). Developing a personal theory of counseling: A brief guide for students. *TCA Journal, 21*(1), 103–104. doi:10.1080/15564223.1993.12034415

5 DIVERSITY COURSES

INTRODUCTION

This course goes by many names: Cultural Diversity, Counseling Diverse Populations, Multicultural Counseling, or Cultural Diversity and Advocacy. Regardless of the name, the course content can be difficult for some professors and students. This course provides an opportunity for students to encounter the cultural context of relationships. The course touches on subjects such as culture, ethnicity, nationality, age, gender, sexual orientation, mental and physical characteristics, education, family values, religious and spiritual values, socioeconomic status, and unique characteristics of individuals, couples, families, ethnic groups, and communities.

COURSE DESCRIPTION

The emphasis of this course is on developing knowledge, skills, and attitudes for building more effective therapeutic relationships with persons different from the student. Characteristics such as race, culture, gender, sexual orientation, physical disability, and religious preference will be explored within the class. Substantial attention will also be given to helping students develop awareness of their own values, attitudes, and beliefs that may influence the way they interact with individuals in a diverse society. This course is important for students because it provides students the opportunity to encounter individuals and beliefs that may be different than their own, which in turn promotes self-exploration and awareness of biases and attitudes toward differentness. With counseling being a largely White and middle-class activity, cultural competency happens when students can free themselves from viewing counseling and clients from "Western social cultural" norms (Sue & Sue, 1997).

The Association for Multicultural Counseling and Development (AMCD) lists multicultural counseling competencies grouped by attitudes, beliefs, knowledge, and skills. These competencies are grouped into areas related to awareness of our own cultural values and biases, awareness of clients' worldviews, and culturally appropriate intervention strategies. This course will provide students an opportunity to reflect on internalized messages regarding other groups as well as challenge students to bring behaviors and attitudes into alignment with professional standards.

COURSE OBJECTIVES

The main objective of this course is that students understand and demonstrate the content, knowledge, skills, and dispositions necessary to help clients from all backgrounds. This course seeks to spark students' awareness of and ability to counsel clients across a range of diversity. More specific objectives of which students will demonstrate mastery are the following topics:

1. Theories of identity development
2. Multicultural and pluralistic trends
3. The nature of several topics such as prejudice, bias, processes of oppression, and discrimination
4. Theories of multicultural counseling
5. Multicultural competencies
6. Individual, couple, family, group, and community strategies for working with diverse populations and ethnic groups

7. Issues of social justice and the counselor's role
8. Awareness of one's own culture
9. Ethical and legal considerations

Other objectives specific to Council for Accreditation of Counseling and Related Educational Programs (CACREP)-accredited programs that this course is designed to meet are the CACREP Core Standards for social and cultural diversity. The following standards should be covered in this course:

1. Multicultural and pluralistic characteristics within and among diverse groups nationally and internationally
2. Theories and models of multicultural counseling, cultural identity development, and social justice and advocacy
3. Multicultural counseling competencies
4. The impact of heritage, attitudes, beliefs, understandings, and acculturative experiences on an individual's views of others
5. The effects of power and privilege for counselors and clients
6. Help-seeking behaviors of diverse clients
7. The impact of spiritual beliefs on clients' and counselors' worldviews
8. Strategies for identifying and eliminating barriers, prejudices, and processes of intentional and unintentional oppression and discrimination
9. Ethical and culturally relevant strategies for promoting resilience and optimum development and wellness across the life span
10. Ethical and culturally relevant strategies for establishing and maintaining in-person and technology-assisted relationships
11. Cultural factors relevant to clinical mental health counseling
12. Legal and ethical considerations specific to clinical mental health counseling

13. Legal and ethical considerations specific to school counseling
14. Techniques of personal/social counseling in school settings (CACREP, 2016)

MUST-COVER TOPICS

For counselors in training, gaining multicultural awareness and skills involves inward and outward growth. Students must embark, or at least be willing to, on the journey to know the self and then be willing to let that knowledge of self influence the therapeutic process. Students are at the beginning stages of a lifelong process of grappling with the process of interacting with clients in a therapeutic setting who may be different than themselves—the grappling process should be one of self-growth. This course alone will not suffice in making students culturally competent counselors. Topics that must be broached in this course should revolve around the following ideas:

1. Culture being at the center of the therapeutic relationship
2. Worldview
3. Language
4. Leveraging differences
5. Self-awareness
6. Counseling relationship
7. Advocacy
8. Religion
9. Spirituality

Culture being at the center of the therapeutic relationship is an important concept for students to wrestle with as they explore the concepts of this course. Within the therapeutic relationship, the client and counselor both bring in their own cultures. Though the natural pull of this course is toward making students understand cultures that are different from their own, it is also important to start with understanding the self. By understanding the self, students will explore their own beliefs, values, attitudes, and behaviors, essentially making the *other* more obvious and highlighting potential growth areas.

Garrett McAuliffe and Associates (2008) described "worldview" to mean "a set of principles that determines how life is lived and how people think, feel, and act" (p. 267). These principles can be influenced by how individuals identify from a gender perspective, current income or income potential, age, race, and so forth. It is important for students to be in touch with their own worldviews and how they impact relationships. The awareness of one's own worldview allows for acknowledgment of one's own cultural conditioning, which aids in developing culturally appropriate strategies when working with individuals.

Language plays a major role in the therapeutic relationship. There is a particular language that is spoken within the therapeutic relationship—each client is a bit different in use of sarcasm or the pace and tone of voice, for example. Also, there is a language that is spoken outside of the therapeutic relationship—the language the client and counselor speak with their family and peers. This language contains culturally specific terms and emphases. It is important for students to understand this difference and be interested and invested in finding a mutual understanding of language or communication patterns.

Other topics that may be important for students to touch on briefly throughout the duration of this course are:

1. Understanding power
2. Understanding therapeutic presence
3. Making culturally appropriate diagnosis
4. Understanding terms such as "racism," "prejudice," and "discrimination"
5. Privilege

6. Becoming an ally
7. How parenting looks across cultures
8. Cultural attitudes toward mental health
9. Racial microaggressions
10. Substance usage

When working with specific cultural groups, it is also important to consider the demographic details and the family and cultural values.

PERSONAL EXPERIENCE

Teaching Approach

When teaching this course, we strongly suggest considering the following: (a) Do your own work around diversity in your own life; (b) Students' life experiences play a major role in their perceptions and understanding in this course; (c) This topic is uncomfortable for some students or even has been avoided for most of their lives; (d) There may be arguments or tension in this course, which is not always a bad thing; (e) This class can jeopardize your self-care, so please pay attention to how much energy you are putting into this course.

After agreeing to take on a course such as this one, rely on professors who have taught this course before to guide you through their process of how to approach various topics in the course. If you are a new professor, it is important to gain important information about the students such as how many students usually take this course, what are the prerequisites, what are some usual areas of tension for students, and what class assignments worked or did not work.

The material covered in this course can cause some students to seek shelter in the comfort of their minds by remaining quiet so as not to offend others or overshare in an attempt to express themselves. Therefore, normalizing this process for students is important at the onset of the course. Articulating these sentiments and exploring students' fears or reservations with expressing themselves freely in the course is important. Also, creating course rules that specifically state how students would like to treat confidentiality and respect for differing opinions is also important.

Student Experience

As mentioned previously, students' life experiences play a significant role in their perceptions and understanding of the course material. Also, topics covered in this course may be uncomfortable for some students. Tensions rise when students encounter difficult subjects regarding issues in diversity because it is a deeply personal subject that may uncover values and opinions that differ from others. What makes this class particularly tense is that these "others" are the classmates whom students share educational experiences with, share notes with, get dinner after class with, but also consider close friends in some cases. Sharing thoughts on issues of diversity that may change the way friends see each other can be a stressful situation, which is why normalizing this process and openly discussing these issues in class can be beneficial.

Course Preparation

Preparing for this class starts with the self. It is imperative to explore issues that may be covered in class that could cause issues or hang-ups for you throughout the experience. Speaking with colleagues, peers, your personal counselor, or even a supervisor can help uncover some unfinished business that could help you be a more effective educator. Regarding preparing the students for this experience, this also needs to be done early on in the course experience. Starting with the first class, it may be beneficial for students to know the purpose behind specific assignments and to facilitate students processing their hesitations or excitement for these assignments.

Self-disclosing your hesitations and excitement for assignments may also help to normalize the experience as well as humanize you. It can be easy to see the professor as culturally competent in every way as opposed to a clinician and educator who is consistently working on competency. Also, disclosing times where you may not have been the most culturally responsible with your words and actions may provide an invitation for students to be vulnerable in their expressions and course experience.

Advice

The part of this course that we enjoy the most is the acknowledgment of the fact that personal learning and growing are a lifelong process by students. We also enjoy being a part of the process where students can become vulnerable in class or with themselves and acknowledge their bias, power, and privilege. Helping students become personally responsible for their thoughts and feelings regarding the course material are also highlights of teaching this course. We found that, as African American men, students have preconceived notions about our background or our journey through life. Being open and vulnerable with students and helping students to feel comfortable asking questions out of curiosity have a direct effect on their comfortability when asking questions to mock clients throughout the course. Regarding being men of color, our experience as students as well as professors in this course was one of pressure to speak for our race when topics broached African American culture. We could almost feel the eyes in the class shift in our direction. Mentioning this personal experience at the onset of the course helps normalize this process for students who may at times feel the pressure to speak for their culture. It also sheds light on the experience so that others in the class do not knowingly or unknowingly pressure individuals into this scenario. However, it is also important to provide space for students who feel comfortable enough to share similarities between the course materials and their cultural experience.

COURSE CONSIDERATIONS

Additional Textbooks

- *Multicultural Issues in Counseling: New Approaches to Diversity*, by Courtland C. Lee (2018)
- *Counseling the Culturally Diverse: Theory and Practice*, by Derald Wing Sue and David Sue (2019)
- *Diversity in Couple and Family Therapy: Ethnicities, Sexualities, and Socioeconomics*, by Shalonda Kelly (2016)
- *Diversity in Counseling*, by Robyn Brammer (2011)
- *Cultural Diversity: A Primer for the Human Services*, by Jerry V. Diller (2018)
- *Becoming a Multiculturally Competent Counselor*, by Changming Duan and Chris Brown (2015)
- *Assessing and Treating Culturally Diverse Clients: A Practical Guide*, by Freddy A. Paniagua (2014)

Mock Schedule

A potential course schedule may look like the example in Exhibit 5.1.

EXHIBIT 5.1   Diversity Course: Mock Schedule

Week	Topic
1	In-Class Cultural Experience Review Syllabus
2	Intro to Multicultural Counseling Foundational Concepts
3	Privilege White Guilt and Anger
4	ISMS Critical Race Theory Identity Development
5	Implicit Biases Generational Pain Sex, Gender, and Sexual Orientation
6	Ability and Aging Spirituality and Religion Social Class and SES
7	Developing Multicultural Competence Working With Microaggressions
8	Communication Rapport Building, Broaching, and Assessment
9	Interventions, Empowerment, and Advocacy
10	Group presentations: Cultural Scrapbooks
11	Processing Discussion Celebration of Class

SES, socioeconomic status.

COURSE ASSIGNMENTS

Reflective Journals

Reflective journals can be classified as Reflective Journal 1, Reflective Journal 2, and Reflective Journal 3.

The purpose of the reflective journal is to provide a critical response to a topic within the weekly readings.

Journals should be three to five double-spaced pages. Here are the topics and required responses for each of the reflective journals.

Reflective Journal 1. Topic: Importance of Developing Multicultural Competence

For Reflective Journal 1, address the following points:

- Provide a brief synopsis of the main points on pages_____.
- Provide your thoughts and responses to the information. How is this information relevant to your own life and learning experiences? Additionally, how might this information be relevant to your career and growth as a counselor?

Reflective Journal 2. Topic: Social Justice Advocacy
For Reflective Journal 2, address the following points:

- Provide a brief synopsis of the main points on pages_____.
- Develop a Personal Social Justice Plan based on _____.

Reflective Journal 3. Topic: Applications of Counseling Theory Across Cultures

For Reflective Journal 3, address the following points:

- Provide a brief synopsis of the main points on pages _____.
- Give examples of conventional Western assumptions in counseling theories.

Cultural Movie Review

Choose a movie (professor's discretion regarding type of movie). Your review should be at least _____ pages. Address the following in your critical response: (a) synopsis of the movie, (b) cultural groups addressed in the movie, (c) issues/dilemmas presented in relation to these cultural groups, (d) sources to discuss the information in the film that appeared accurate or inaccurate, (e) social justice issues presented in the movie, and (f) ways in which you would engage in advocacy related to the theme/topic presented in the film.

Culture of Origin Paper

The purpose of this assignment is to explore your culture of origin. This paper will demand an exploration of your race and ethnicity, to the extent that you know. Additionally, this paper will provide an opportunity for you to clarify and elaborate on your cultural values, beliefs, traditions, and elements of worldview(s) that have been passed down from generation to generation, up to the present time. Include, without limiting yourself to, such areas as (a) the causes and nature of mental health illness related to your culture, (b) notions of spirituality/religion, (c) the degree of responsibility that an individual has over life choices, (d) what relationships with nature look like, (e) examples of hierarchical undertones of familial relationships, (f) attitudes regarding education, (g) approaches to acknowledging, understanding, and expressing emotions, and (h) cultural influences on your worldview.

Identity Analysis Presentation

Students will apply one or two models of culture identity development to their own lives and development. Students may choose the model(s) that they feel are most personally relevant. In the application of the model, students must provide an overview of the model and its relevance to their lives and development. Students should be prepared to present 15 to 20 slides (if using PowerPoint) to the class.

REFERENCES

Council for Accreditation of Counseling and Related Educational Programs. (2016). *2016 CACREP standards*. Retrieved from https://www.cacrep.org/for-programs/2016-cacrep-standards

McAuliffe, G., & Associates. (2008). *Culturally alert counseling. A comprehensive introduction.* Thousand Oaks, CA: SAGE.

Sue, D. W., & Sue, D. (1997). Barriers to effective cross-cultural counseling. *Journal of Counseling Psychology, 24*(5), 420–429. doi:10.1037/0022-0167.24.5.420

LIFE-SPAN DEVELOPMENT COURSES

INTRODUCTION

Life-span development courses cover the human experience from conception to death. Counselor educators use a holistic approach encompassing the physiological, cognitive, emotional, cultural, and social changes clients experience. Specifically, the course provides an in-depth study of human development theories, biological and environmental foundations, cultural influences, and lifestyles in human development. Practically, the course will also focus on how these aspects of human development impact the counseling process.

COURSE DESCRIPTION

This course is separated into stages of human development. Typically, each class is dedicated to a specific stage. Within each stage are biological and social cultural aspects of human development that are covered. The course may start by covering the history, theories, and research strategies involved in studying life-span development. This orientates students to the topic and prepares them to dive deeper into developmental theories. This course covers well-known life-span development theories such as:

- Freud's psychosexual developmental theory
- Erikson's psychosocial developmental theory

- John Watson and B. F. Skinner's behavioral child development theory
- Piaget's cognitive developmental theory
- Bowlby's attachment theory
- Bandura's social learning theory
- Vygotsky's sociocultural theory
- Kohlberg's theory of moral development

This course is important for students because it helps them develop a life-span perspective in counseling. Clients do not live in a vacuum. They face unique challenges depending on their contexts and how they interact with those contexts. The life-span perspective helps counselors contextualize their clients' experiences. It can be a useful therapeutic tool.

It is also important because it helps students to reflect on their own life course. In each class, students cannot help but to analyze their life from that day's developmental stage and from different theoretical perspectives. In addition to their own lives, they reflect upon their parents, children, and partners. By this course, students have already been taking a techniques class where they have to practice skills or a group class where they have to participate in a therapeutic group. Experiences are starting to align, and they may be seeing their behaviors, perspectives, and the reasons for these more clearly.

COURSE OBJECTIVES

Upon completion of this course, students will have an understanding of the terminology used in life-span development. This includes the terms used in the theories mentioned in the course description earlier, as well as definitions and concepts appropriate to each stage of development. Students will also learn the basic principles of research, neurobiology, and ecological aspects of life-span development. They will discuss some ethical and legal considerations when working with clients from different stages of development: children, adolescents, adults, and the elderly. Students will identify and explain theories of life-span development, including family development as well as individual development. They will demonstrate their understanding of the family life cycle, aging, and family wellness. They will explain social and cultural diversity across the life span to include special needs of individuals and families. They will also identify and explain features of social development, such as family, environment, exceptionality, vocational and developmental crises, disability, and psychopathology relating to both normal and abnormal behavior. Students will demonstrate the ability to differentiate between diagnoses and developmentally appropriate reactions related to the effects of crisis, trauma, and disasters on individuals of all ages as well as the family system. Students will also discuss how addictions and addictive behaviors, including prevention, intervention, and treatment of addictions, influence individuals and families across the life span. Finally, students will discuss death, dying, and bereavement and their effects on the individual and family across the life span.

MUST-COVER TOPICS

It is beyond the scope of this book to explain in detail each topic covered in this course. However, we briefly describe some of these topics to provide a general understanding of their importance to the course.

Nature Versus Nurture

This topic is a common debate juxtaposing the extent to which certain aspects of human behavior are a result of inherited or acquired influences. Nature holds that behavior is influenced by hereditary information received from parents at conception. Nurture insists that behavior is influenced by physical and social forces.

Periods of Development

Development is separated into periods defined by an individual's age. Each period has its own milestones and developmental experiences. The course covers the following periods of development:

- Prenatal period: conception to birth
- Infancy and toddlerhood: birth to 2 years of age
- Early childhood: 2 years of age to 6
- Middle childhood: 6 to 11 years old
- Adolescence: 11 to 18 years old
- Early adulthood: 18 to 40 years of age
- Middle adulthood: 40 to 65 years old
- Late adulthood: 65 years old to death

Each class can focus on a different period of development. Counselor educators will view each stage from different theoretical lenses as well as focus on the physical and emotional changes occurring at each stage.

Domains of Development

The domains of development covered in this course are physical, cognitive, emotional, and social. The physical domain covers the development of physical changes, such as growing bigger and stronger and motor skills, both gross and fine. The physical domain also covers the development of an individual's five senses and how he or she uses them. The cognitive domain includes the development of intellect and creativity. It also covers how individuals process information, think, pay attention, remember things, build situational awareness, and make plans and follow through with those plans. The emotional and social domain focuses on how individuals understand and manage their emotions. It also focuses on how individuals build empathy for the feelings of others and how they interact with others.

Continuous and Discontinuous Development

Continuous and discontinuous development refer to an individual's view of development. Some theorists believe that development is a smooth, gradual process. Individuals gradually add more of the same types of skills. This is an example of continuous development. Other theorists believe development takes place in discontinuous stages. Individuals change and grow rapidly as they step up to a new level. Then they change very little for a while once they reach that level. With each new step, individuals interpret and respond to the world in a reorganized, qualitatively different way.

Major Theories

In short, theories were developed to show how individuals grow from birth to adults. The theories explain how this growth is normal and can become abnormal. Here is a brief description of those theories.

Freud's (1989) psychosexual developmental theory proposed that an individual's personality develops during early childhood (2–6 years old). In that time, individuals go through stages for which they need support from their primary caregivers. Without this support, individuals can become stuck or fixated in that stage.

Erikson's (1993) psychosocial developmental theory expanded Freud's theory from only childhood to across the entire life span. He also highlighted the social experiences within development instead of just the sexual experiences. In short, Erikson explained that our interactions with others affect our sense of self, our ego identity. Each individual has different checkpoints throughout his or her development; he identified eight checkpoints or stages. Within these stages is a conflict or a task that needs to be completed. If the task is not completed, an individual's ego identity is negatively impacted. Complete the task and the individual's ego remains intact.

Behavioral child development theorists, such as John Watson, believed that a child's environment shapes his or her behavior. Watson (2017) believed that he could train infants to become specialists in any field by exposing them to certain environmental forces for an extended time. He believed that children can be conditioned to become any type of person.

Piaget's (1976) cognitive developmental theory saw children as little scientists who are constantly experimenting, observing, and learning about the world. Their interactions with the world are how they learn. He believed that children move through four different stages: sensorimotor, preoperational, concrete operational, and formal operational. His theory focuses on cognitive processes and abilities.

Bowlby's (1978) attachment theory suggests that mental health and behavioral problems are influenced by children's attachment to their primary caregivers. He suggests that children are born preprogramed to attach to others, and the circumstances of that attachment influence their style of attaching to others. There are different attachment styles, including secure, avoidant, ambivalent/anxious, and disorganized attachment. In secure attachments children feel safe with their caregivers; seen, and soothed. As they grow, they can use their caregivers as a home base while they explore the world. Individuals with avoidant attachments may pull away from needing anything from anyone because their parents may have been emotionally unavailable. Individuals with ambivalent/anxious attachment are often confused and insecure, distrustful, and also clingy because their caregivers' support was unpredictable. Individuals with a disorganized attachment may develop this style as a result of childhood abuse, physical and/or emotional. Their source of safety and comfort are the very individuals abusing them. This style causes individuals to detach from themselves often, but especially in times of stress. Their insecurities may leave them emotionally desperate in their relationships.

Bandura's social learning theory suggests that individuals learn by observing one another. There is a continuous reciprocal interaction between behaviors, cognitions, and the environment, according to Bandura and Walters (1977). They went on to define the term "reciprocal determinism," meaning that an individual's behavior and the world cause each other or behavior causes environment. Essentially, Bandura believed that behavior is learned from the environment through the process of observation.

Vygotsky's sociocultural theory describes learning as a social and cultural process. Cognition is developed through social interaction. According to Vygotsky (1997), everything is learned first through interaction with others and then integrated into the individual's mental structure; interpsychological, then intrapsychological. Vygotsky also introduced the term "zone of proximal development," which explains the learning process. He explained that individuals have a comfortable zone, or area of knowledge, but need help and social interaction to develop fuller understanding.

Kohlberg's (1981) theory of moral development holds that an individual's moral reasoning develops in stages. He explained that there are six identifiable stages that can be classified into three levels. The three levels are preconventional, conventional, and postconventional. Kohlberg (1981) explained that an individual could not jump stages but had to go from one to another, in order. An individual develops insight as he or she faces cognitive conflicts at each stage.

Developmental Neuroscience

There are two areas of developmental neuroscience: cognitive and social. Developmental cognitive neuroscience focuses on the relationship between brain activity and cognitive processing and behavioral patterns. The area incorporates psychology, biology, neuroscience, and medicine. Developmental social neuroscience focuses on the relationship between brain activity and emotional and social development.

Genetic and Environmental Foundations

This topic alone could be its own course. It is packed with content that some students may find interesting while others find unimportant. When covering this area of life-span development, counselor educators can focus on areas such as:

- Genetic foundations: genes, chromosomes, DNA
- Meiosis and mitosis
- Chromosomal abnormalities
- Reproductive choices
- Genetic counseling
- Reproductive technologies
- Adoption
- Environmental contexts of development, such as family, socioeconomic status, poverty/affluence, neighborhoods, schools, and cultural contexts

Prenatal Development, Birth, and Newborn Babies

This topic is another area of life-span development that could be its own course. Briefly, here are some sections in this area on which to spend time in class:

- Conception: counselors may find themselves in the position to explain conception as it results

from intercourse. This section facilitates a
discussion of that process.
- Periods of prenatal development such as the
germinal, embryonic, and fetal periods. The fetal
period is separated into three trimesters, which
are important to cover as well.
- Prenatal environmental influences such as
teratogens and teratogenic substances such
as drugs, tobacco, alcohol, radiation and
environmental pollution, and infectious diseases.
- Childbirth, which is a subject that may require
a considerable amount of class time to discuss.
This is especially so if some students are eager
to share their birth stories. When covering this
subject, it may be helpful to focus on the stages
of childbirth, the baby's adaptation to labor and
delivery, and the Apgar scale. Additionally, it
may be fitting to discuss the different approaches
to childbirth, such as natural, home delivery, and
birthing centers.
- Newborn capabilities such as crying and
developing senses.
- Adapting to family unit, involving areas such as
hormonal changes and adjusting.

PERSONAL EXPERIENCE

Teaching Approach

In general, we approach each course with an attempt to
teach experientially and relationally. We enjoy discussions
and activities that help students integrate the information into their way of working with clients. However, we
have found that teaching this course in that way can be
challenging. When teaching the class experientially dominate, discussions lead the class astray at times. This was
especially true when discussing hot button topics such
as attachment, child birth, child rearing, and navigating

Erikson's stages of development. These topics tend to cause some students to share and overshare their experiences or perspectives. These discussions, while rich, can get in the way of covering the course content. So, we have adopted an old-fashioned lecture style with limited space for small discussion points and short activities. Quantifiably, we dedicate 90% of the class to covering content in the lecture, 5% to discussions, and 5% to activities. Even with these classes being heavily lecture based, the content invites students to be reflective. Wherever we can, we ask students to take a moment and reflect on their lives. We do not always ask them to share, but these reflections usually drive their questions. Inviting students to be reflective is especially impactful when advanced students are taking this course. Students in practicum or internship can also reflect on their clients' development and how it influences the therapeutic relationship. There is a palpable tension when teaching this course between personal discussion and covering the course content. The content is important because this topic is an important part of students' comprehensive exams and licensure exams. How counselor educators manage this tension influences students' experience in the course.

Student Experience

The feedback we have gotten from students is consistent with our experience as counselor educators. When discussions dominate the class, students can sometimes feel as though the classes are less productive and helpful. When we are more intentional about controlling the process of class, students appreciate the lectures and feel prepared to work with clients from a life-span perspective. Similar to the professional orientation courses, there is a great amount of content to cover. In addition to the content, the assignments may be reflective in nature. Students experience this course with some anxiety. Some have concerns about taking in the information in a way they can use it to work with clients. We have noticed that students struggle with the content when they try to learn the information as if it were a subject like math or science. The content needs to be learned like a language, and it needs to be reflected upon and filtered through students' lived experiences. Doing this is scary for some students who see the course as an intimidating reflection of their entire development since birth. Students who are parents often reflect on how they have raised their children and the negative impact they may have had on their children's psyches. Although this class is packed with content, there is potential for students to be emotionally affected by the topics of the day.

Course Preparation

On average, we create between 170 and 180 pages of lecture notes for this course. This includes links to videos, extra graphs and figures, additional information, and personal examples. Preparing for this course takes us a considerable amount of time. The challenge is whittling the content down to the most essential content that can be covered during the class period. If the course is on Thursday evening, we begin preparing on Monday. We start by reading the book chapter assigned and then relevant literature. We combine these sources to create the lecture outline. This outline has three or four times more information than will be covered in class because we account for questions. For example, when discussing child birthing options, there are different rules and options available to women in the area. Students may have specific questions about hospitals or birthing centers. The more personalized we can make the lectures, the more useful they become.

For each class, we present the lecture outline based on the assigned readings and relevant literature. Then we select the most essential components of the outline to make the PowerPoint lecture presentation. When creating the presentation, we pay attention for any content or process that could be learned by watching a video or through a guest speaker. For example, the reproductive process is better explained through the use of a video so students can see sperm and egg developing into a fetus, following the process until birth. We add any videos or other digital content into the presentation. Then, if a guest speaker is planned for the day, we contact that individual and confirm his or her appearance. With intentionality and planning, counselor educators can manage the amount of information presented and discussed in each class.

Nuts and Bolts

We do not rely on the in-class lectures to cover all of the information on a given topic. Some of the topics would take three class periods to fully cover. Instead, we use the online course resources to create modules, practice quizzes, and discussion posts to enhance student learning. Information that does not make it into the presentation can be posed as a discussion question for students. Class discussions that would take up lecture time can now still take place online. Doing this allows students who learn from conversations and peer interaction to receive this experience.

One of the most meaningful assignments students complete in this course is their personal development paper. Students choose a time in their lives when they might have sought counseling. Then, they discuss this experience and conceptualize it through three developmental approaches. It is a powerful and reflective assignment that encourages students to process their lives. The work to manage grading this assignment as well as the others starts in the first class. We take our time in those early classes to explain to students what we are looking for and how to write in American Psychological Association (APA) Style using a professional voice. We follow up this discussion before writing assignments are due. We also discuss the rubrics to explain to students how they can score a high grade by following the rubrics. Grading the assignments in this course is challenging because of how personal some of the assignments are for students. The personal development assignment asks for five to seven pages of text. However, students often begin writing and pour their hearts out in a 10- to 15-page document. Sometimes they discuss past trauma, racism, relationships issues, and tragedies. It is difficult to give a student who appears to have grown personally while in the process of writing the paper, but struggled writing professionally and technically. Counselor educators need to consider this dilemma when teaching this course.

In addition to being mindful of how to maintain grades for emotionally charged assignments, counselor educators may benefit from considering cultural ideas of normal and abnormal development. For example, not all cultures see emotional and financial independence as being the ultimate mark of health. Also, not all close familial relationships are enmeshed. Different cultures go through the developmental stages in their own way. It is important for counselor educators to acknowledge cultural differences throughout this course.

Advice

Heavy content courses have similar pitfalls, such as bombarding students with information, teaching at a distance, and not training the person of the therapist, to name a few. Counselor educators should be wary of making those mistakes when teaching this course. Additionally, counselor educators should be mindful of how discussions are influencing student learning. Occasionally, heavy content courses can be filled with students who can communicate their experiences without getting sidetracked. Other times, one student may share his or her birth story, and then everyone else in the class starts to share and overshare to the dismay of students who wanted to learn about something else in that day's reading. Counselor educators should also avoid overlecturing students. This can look like PowerPoint presentations that have upward of 50 slides. Students may open that PowerPoint file and make audible groans. Counselor educators should be mindful of their biases regarding normal development. In that same vein, counselor educators should be aware of the power they hold in class when identifying a behavior, cognition, or emotion as normal or abnormal. Some advice for counselor educators teaching this course for the first time includes the following:

- Consider multicultural perspectives regarding normal and abnormal.
- Give students a venue to discuss topics that may not fit into a class length.
- Prepare students regarding the APA Style of writing and specific rubric requirements.
- Prepare for class extensively, creating a course outline that plans the class hour by hour.
- Discuss the personal reflective process involved in this course.
- Find videos and diagrams to describe prenatal, biological topics.
- Tie childhood developmental experiences toward psychopathology when possible.
- Help students integrate the life-span perspective into their clinical work.

COURSE CONSIDERATIONS

Additional Textbooks

The following are textbooks to consider when teaching this course:

- *Development Through the Lifespan*, by Laura E. Berk (2017)

- *Lenses: Applying Lifespan Development Theories in Counseling*, by Kurt L. Kraus (2008)
- *Counseling Individuals Through the Lifespan*, by Daniel W. Wong, Kimberly R. Hall, Cheryl A. Justice, and Lucy Wong Hernandez (2020)
- *Lives Across Cultures: Cross-Cultural Human Development*, by Harry W. Gardiner (2017)

Mock Schedule

Exhibit 6.1 is an example of a potential course schedule if the book was *Development Through the Lifespan*, by Laura E. Berk (2017).

EXHIBIT 6.1 Life-Span Development Course: Mock Schedule

Date	Course Content	Readings* and Assignments
Aug 20	Introduction to Course Discussion of Assignments and Grading	Syllabus
Aug 27	History, Theory, and Research Strategies	Chapter 1
Sep 3	Labor Day Holiday	No Class
Sep 10	Genetic and Environmental Foundations	Chapter 2
Sep 17	Prenatal Development, Birth, the Newborn Baby, and Attachment	Chapter 3
Sep 24	Infancy and Toddlerhood: The First Two Years	Chapters 4–6
Oct 1	Early Childhood: Two to Six Years	Chapter 7

(*continued*)

EXHIBIT 6.1 Life-Span Development Course: Mock Schedule (*continued*)

Date	Course Content	Readings* and Assignments
Oct 8	Midterm	Chapters 1–7
Oct 15	Middle Childhood: Six to Eleven Years	Chapter 8
Oct 22	Adolescence: The Transition to Adulthood	Chapters 9, 10
Oct 29	Early Adulthood	Chapters 11, 12
Nov 5	Middle Adulthood	Chapters 13, 14
Nov 12	Late Adulthood	Chapters 15, 16, 17
Nov 19	The End of Life	Chapters 18, 19
Nov 26	Case Conceptualization Presentations	
Dec 3	Cumulative Final	Chapters 1–19

*Listed readings refer to Berk, L. E. (2017). *Development through the lifespan*. Boston, MA: Pearson.

COURSE ASSIGNMENTS

Personal Development Paper

You will assess and write a paper reviewing your experiences during a major stage of your development (early, middle, late childhood; early or late adolescence; or early or middle adulthood). Your paper should address significant systemic and environmental factors that affected your development, functioning, and behavior. The paper should also address significant issues (e.g., addictions, trauma, violence, family dynamics, sexuality, socioeconomic standing) and life events that you experienced during the stage of development which you selected, and the effect these events and issues had on you at that time and that may currently still have. Issues that could be addressed include biological, psychological, social, and spiritual development, sexuality, drugs/substance use, peer relationships, body image, and family dynamics. Address how issues of diversity affected your development. Address how your life experiences at the stage of development on which you are focusing, shaped and have influenced your life. Identify and include a discussion of at least three theories that you must integrate into your paper. Demonstrate how the theories can be used to explain your experience with your development and related behavior. As an example, you may want to discuss how social learning theory may explain your involvement with certain friends. The paper should be in APA Style, five to seven pages in length, not including the front page and reference list.

Case Conceptualization Through the Lens of a Developmental Theory

You will find and select a case study to read and conceptualize using a developmental theory. This paper will address (a) significant systemic and environmental factors that affect development, functioning, and behavior and (b) the biological, neurological, and physiological factors that affect human development, functioning, and behavior. The case conceptualization should be five to seven typewritten pages, including a title page, body of the paper, and a reference page. Five references must be used. One reference can be the textbook, and the others must be journal articles no more than 10 years old. APA writing style must be used.

Adult Attachment Interview

Students will interview a parent about his or her experience and observations about his or her child. The interview takes 30 minutes, but students should allow for 45 minutes total. Students are to avoid interviewing a person experiencing major life stressors such as domestic violence, recent or planned divorce/separation, severe illness in self or child, homelessness, or miscarriage. Students must consult with the professor to receive permission to interview that parent. Here are the questions you will ask the primary caregiver of a particular child:

1. Tell me about what you first noticed about _____ when he or she was born or in the first few weeks. (Or, if the child is adopted or a foster child, "when you first met.")
2. What kind of child is _____? Or what do you notice about his or her personality?
3. What are his or her strengths and/or challenges?
4. How would you characterize your relationship with _____? Has this changed over time?
5. What kind of adult do you hope _____ will become?
6. Do you notice anything about your childhood or upbringing that affects your parenting?
7. Can you provide me with two adjectives that describe your mother when you were little and give me an example of why you chose these words?
8. Can you provide me with two adjectives that describe your father when you were little and give me an example of why you chose these words?
9. Did this conversation stimulate other thoughts that you might want to add before we finish?

Students will then reflect upon their experience and then answer the following questions:

1. What themes are present in your interviewee's view of his or her child? Support your analysis

with short nonidentifying quotes from the interview.

2. Do you see any connection between attachment theory and the comments the interviewee made during the interview? Why, or why not? Give examples to support your thoughts.

3. Include other nonattachment comments as needed. Be sure to include a short introduction, including the general setting and nonidentifying information about the person you interviewed.

REFERENCES

Bandura, A., & Walters, R. H. (1977). *Social learning theory* (Vol. 1). Englewood Cliffs, NJ: Prentice-Hall.

Bowlby, J. (1978). Attachment theory and its therapeutic implications. *Adolescent Psychiatry, 6,* 5–33. Retrieved from https://psycnet.apa.org/record/1982-00026-001

Erikson, E. H. (1993). *Childhood and society.* New York, NY: W. W. Norton.

Freud, S. (1989). *The psychopathology of everyday life.* New York, NY: W. W. Norton.

Kohlberg, L. (1981). *Essays on moral development* (Vol. 1, pp. 409–412). San Francisco, CA: Harper & Row.

Piaget, J. (1976). Piaget's theory. In B. Inhelder & H. H. Chipman (Eds.), *Piaget and his school* (pp. 11–23). Berlin, Germany: Springer-Verlag.

Vygotsky, L. S. (1997). *The collected works of LS Vygotsky: Problems of the theory and history of psychology* (Vol. 3). New York, NY: Springer Science & Business Media.

Watson, J. B. (2017). *Behaviorism.* London, UK: Routledge.

7 | COUNSELING TECHNIQUES COURSES

INTRODUCTION

In order for students to explore and understand counseling techniques, most counseling programs provide a sequence of courses that build on each other. These courses are called by several different names, but for the purposes of this chapter, we use the following names: Methods of Counseling, Advanced Techniques, and Prepracticum. In each of these courses, the difficulty level increases for the student, and the lessons build from the previous class. These classes provide students with the building blocks for strong relationships with clients as well as help students to narrow their focus on a counselor identity. This chapter consolidates the three courses listed here into a cohesive explanation of the counseling technique educational process.

COURSE DESCRIPTION

The Counseling Techniques courses are designed to teach basic to advanced clinical counseling skills and help students crystalize the counseling theories and methods through experiencing mock therapeutic cases or sessions. Students are introduced to the foundational counseling skills that will be necessary for success in more advanced Counseling Techniques courses. These are primarily experiential courses that highlight practicing skills, didactic information, as well as processes the students experience when entering a therapeutic relationship.

COURSE OBJECTIVES

The objectives of the Counseling Techniques courses are to help students with the following:

- Cultivate a working understanding of each theory studied in the counseling theories course
- Understand differences within the techniques that are unique to each major counseling theory
- Think critically about skills that go into conceptualizing client issues theoretically
- Understand and demonstrate basic to advanced methods of establishing a therapeutic relationship in the counseling process
- Demonstrate interviewing, observation, and active listening skills
- Develop a working knowledge of ethical and multicultural competencies related to counseling techniques
- Demonstrate clinical skills such as open communication, reflection of content and feeling, interpretation, confrontation, providing appropriate feedback, and understanding appropriate self-disclosure

MUST-COVER TOPICS

As previously mentioned, the Counseling Techniques courses are usually a sequence of courses that build upon each other. The topics covered in each course, though they may be similar, are slightly different in the way that students respond to the skills. For example, a student in Methods of Counseling during his or her initial mock therapy sessions will respond differently to reflecting a client's feeling as a student in the later stages of the semester in Advanced Techniques. The areas of Methods of Counseling that may need to be covered are as follows:

- Attending to self
- Introducing yourself
- Intentional/clinical observation
- Attending to the client
- Using questions
- Paraphrasing
- Summarizing
- Active listening
- Reflection of feelings
- Reflection of content
- Reflection of process

Advanced Techniques is a little different from the previously mentioned course in the sense that it is an overview of these skills with the addition of fostering the student's exploration into his or her counselor identity. This exploration can cause the student to individualize these techniques and make the usage of the techniques personal to him or her. Students will need to demonstrate understanding of practices of diagnosis, treatment, prevention, and counseling intervention from initial session to termination. The areas of Advanced Techniques that would be important to explore with students are:

- Empathizing
- Self-disclosure
- Providing feedback
- Using silence
- Confrontation

- Reframing
- Goal setting
- Using metaphors
- Using humor
- Scaling
- The suicide questions

Prepracticum uses the information and skills covered in the previous courses with the additional usage of theory-specific techniques. The areas of prepracticum that would be important to explore with students are:

- Dealing with resistance
- How to terminate with a client
- Usage of role-plays in session
- Usage of defense mechanisms
- The empty chair technique
- Spitting in the client's soup
- Usage of models such as the ABC (Antecedent, Beliefs, Consequences) or WDEP (Wants, Doing, Evaluation, and Planning)
- The miracle question
- The termination process

PERSONAL EXPERIENCE

Teaching Approach

The Counseling Techniques courses are difficult to approach because they essentially need to all work cohesively to usher students into their practicums and internships with enough working knowledge base to propel a session forward. However, the courses are unique to the specific professor teaching them. We use experiential exercises within the course to show techniques as opposed to explaining them. This means that any other professor who demonstrates the same technique would highlight different aspects of the technique. This phenomenon is important to mention to students. It is important to have students approach these courses with a beginner's mind, but it is also important to recognize that no technique can be performed perfectly during experiential techniques. Additionally, we approach this course by explaining to students that because our theoretical orientation is embedded in our clinical work, a lot of these demonstrations will have the taste of our style attached. We make it a point to remind students that understanding the technique's purpose is the goal in the course—not judging whether or not they liked their peers' or professors' styles of therapy.

Student Experience

This is one of the first courses where students are able to take what they have learned theoretically and apply it to actual case examples with real thinking and breathing individuals in front of them. This can be anxiety producing for students, and some students, you may notice, become victims to their own expectations. When students make the decision to join the helping profession, these are the courses that they dream about. The Counseling Techniques courses are also one of the best opportunities for faculty to gatekeep students who may not be a good fit for the profession or who may do damage to clients in the future. These factors make the Counseling Techniques courses heavily performance based—so students may excel in courses without a practical component but struggle in the practical aspects of these courses.

Course Preparation

In preparing for these courses, it is important to refresh the clinical skills that may have gone by the wayside in the journey to become who you are now. Going back through old textbooks on basic counseling skills and slowing down the clinical process are important aspects of preparation for this course. Also, have a good handle on which course you are teaching, where it falls in the organization of the Counseling Techniques courses being taught, and at what students will need to be proficient as they matriculate in the program.

COURSE CONSIDERATIONS

Additional Textbooks

- *Theory and Practice of Counseling and Psychotherapy*, by Gerald Corey (2016)
- *Publication Manual of the American Psychological Association* (6th ed.), by American Psychological Association (2011)
- *2014 ACA Code of Ethics*, by American Counseling Association (2014)
- *Advanced Techniques for Counseling and Psychotherapy*, by Christian Conte (2009)
- *Developing Your Theoretical Orientation in Counseling and Psychotherapy*, by Duane A. Halbur and Kimberly Vess Halbur (2011)

Mock Schedules

Methods of Counseling
A potential course schedule may look like the example in Exhibit 7.1, which uses *The Art of Helping*, by Robert R. Carkhuff (2011), as the chosen book.

EXHIBIT 7.1 Methods of Counseling: Mock Schedule

Week	Chapter*	Assignments Due
Aug 20–Aug 26	Introduction and Initial discussion	
Aug 27–Sep 2	Chapter 4: Attending: Involving the Helpee	
Sep 3–Sep 9	Chapter 5: Responding: Facilitating Exploring	
Sep 10–Sep 16	Chapter 5: Responding: Facilitating Exploring	
Sep 17–Sep 23	Chapter 5: Responding: Facilitating Exploring	
Sep 24–Sep 30	Chapter 6: Personalizing: Facilitating Understanding	
Oct 1–Oct 7	Chapter 6: Personalizing: Facilitating Understanding	
Oct 8–Oct 14	Chapter 6: Personalizing: Facilitating Understanding	
Oct 15–Oct 21	Chapter 7: Initiating: Facilitating Acting	
Oct 22–Oct 28	Chapter 8: Recycling the Helping Process	Self-of-Counselor Project/ Presentation Due
Oct 29–Nov 4	Chapter 8: Recycling the Helping Process	
Nov 5–Nov 11	Chapter 2: Structuring Skills	

(*continued*)

EXHIBIT 7.1 Methods of Counseling: Mock Schedule (*continued*)

Week	Chapter*	Assignments Due
Nov 12–Nov 18 Nov 19–Nov 25	Chapter 3: Process Skills	Theoretical Integration Paper Due
Nov 26–Dec 2	Summary Discussion	

*Listed readings refer to Carkhuff, R. (2011). *The art of helping*. Amherst, MA: HRD Press.

Advanced Techniques
Using the text:

> *Advanced Techniques for Counseling and Psychotherapy*, by Christian Conte (2009).

Exhibit 7.2 presents a potential course schedule.

EXHIBIT 7.2 Methods of Counseling: Advanced Techniques Mock Schedule

Week/Date	Objective/Discussion Topics
Week 1 Jan 15	Chapter 1: Introduction*
Week 2 Jan 22	Chapter 1: Introduction
Week 3 Jan 29	Chapter 2: Basic Therapy
Week 4 Feb 5	Chapter 2: Basic Therapy

(*continued*)

EXHIBIT 7.2 Methods of Counseling: Advanced
Techniques Mock Schedule (*continued*)

Week/Date	Objective/Discussion Topics
Week 5 Feb 19	Chapter 3: Metaphor Therapy
Week 6 Feb 26	Chapter 3: Metaphor Therapy
Week 7 Mar 5	Chapter 4: Creative Therapy
Week 8 Mar 12	Chapter 4: Creative Therapy
Week 9 Mar 19	Chapter 5: Projective Therapy
Week 10 Mar 26	Chapter 5: Projective Therapy
Week 11 Apr 9	Chapter 6: Classic Therapy
Week 12 Apr 16	Chapter 6: Classic Therapy
Week 13 May 1	Chapter 6: Classic Therapy
Week 14 May 8	Wrap-Up Discussion

*Listed readings refer to Conte, C. (2009). *Advanced techniques for counseling and psychotherapy*. New York, NY: Springer Publishing Company.

COURSE ASSIGNMENTS

Book Review

Write an 8- to 10-page paper (not including title page, reference page, etc.) on a book related to your theoretical orientation that highlights techniques in counseling. If you are interested in another research-based therapy, submit a book to me for approval.

This paper should focus on the following areas (you do not have to use this order):

(1)   Review the book (brief description, highlights, positives, negatives, learnings, questions upon completion).
(2)   How would you use the theory in your counseling work?
(3)   Which techniques fit/do not fit best with your counseling style? Why?
(4)   What did you learn about your own personal style after completing the book?

Personal Growth Reflection Paper

Students will write about the ways they feel they have grown as a counselor throughout the class. Papers should be three to five pages typed and double spaced. Ten points will be deduced for each page over the page limit. To earn full credit, students should thoroughly answer the bullets outlined here for each paper. Points will be deducted for poor grammar, spelling errors, poor quality of writing, and lack of American Psychological Association (APA) usage. Assignments turned in after the due date will be accepted, but with a loss of five points for each day the paper is late. Submit via Moodle on due date.

- Present opening paragraph (identify for the reader what you will be writing about) *and* closing paragraph (concisely summarize the content of the paper).
- Present your personal description of what counseling is *and* how you would describe it to a client.
- Present skills with which you feel confident *and* rationale (as evidenced by …).

- Present skills you have identified for growth *and* development and rationale (as evidenced by …).
- Specifically address your self-care plan for this semester (separate from your goals).
- What are your goals for this class, *and* how do you plan on achieving them (be specific)?
- Reflect on what you have learned from this class through class activities, assignments, as well as lectures/readings.
- Note your current understanding of the effects of crises, trauma, and culture with the clients you intend to serve.
- Reflect on your experience during in-class practice sessions/round-robin.
- Be sure to include what you learned, what was the most helpful, and the challenges you experienced.
- Discuss the different experiences of being the counselor, the client, and the observer.
- Reflect on at least three of your obstacles to growth professionally and personally that you encountered (e.g., managing emotions; things in your personal life that affected you, whether in class or in practice counseling sessions; work–life balance; feeling underprepared).
- Discuss your theoretical orientation.
- Describe what self-care you engaged in this semester or lack thereof. Discuss why self-care is important.
- Include your goals for continued practice as you move into practicum in the near future *and* how you plan on achieving them (be specific).

Theoretical Integration

Students will write a six-page paper on integrating the concepts of this class with their theoretical perspective.

Of particular use to students will be the information contained in the theories of counseling textbooks, other journal articles, and reference materials. Those six pages are six pages of actual text; with the cover page and references, your paper will be at least eight pages long. The paper must be written in APA format, 6th edition. Include at least five professional, peer-reviewed sources (i.e., professional journals, e.g., the *Journal of Counseling and Development*). Make sure you follow APA format, 6th edition.

Self-of-Counselor Project/Presentation

Each student will be responsible for a 5- to 10-slide PowerPoint presentation using photographs and brief descriptions to answer the following questions:

    (1) Who are you?
    (2) How do you define meaning in your life?
    (3) What is your view of human nature?
    (4) How do you view the process of relationships?
    (5) What represents your style of counseling, or into what do you hope your style develops?

On the assignment due date, you will post your PowerPoint to Moodle, and the class will have the opportunity to learn about you, give feedback, and ask questions.

Taping Role-Plays and Transcript (Twice Throughout the Semester)

This is the dreaded transcribing assignment that is every counselor's rite of passage into the profession. Students will be paired randomly into groups of two. Each student will get a chance to play the client and the counselor for a 30-minute mock skill-practicing session. Students are to record the sessions and transcribe the best 15 minutes of their time as a therapist. Students are expected to meet outside of class time to practice their counseling skills with each other. The session as the counselor should be a minimum of 30 minutes in length.

Choose the best 15 consecutive responses of your video to transcribe. Prepare a verbatim typed script of the best 15 consecutive responses of your interview, noting both counselor and client responses, including nonverbal responses and incidental sounds. Also include an alternative response on each exchange. Recordings will be reviewed by the instructor and evaluated on the student counselor's demonstrated effectiveness in the interview session.

Students will then complete a two-page summary of their counseling session as they evaluate it in its totality. This summary will be added to the end of the transcript. Please be sure to answer the following questions:

- What did I do well?
- In what area(s) do I need improvement?
- How many reflections of feeling did I complete, and how did they affect the session?
- How many questions did I ask, and how did they affect the session?
- What is my overall reaction to the interaction: how was I feeling (i.e., nervous, confident)?

8 CAREER DEVELOPMENT COURSES

INTRODUCTION

This course, unlike theories of counseling or advanced techniques, is sometimes not looked forward to by some students. In the past we have heard several questions and statements along the lines of "This is my first time hearing about career counseling" or "Why do we have to take this course? It shouldn't be on the curriculum." But the question we hear on a consistent basis is "I don't even want to be a career counselor, so why do I have to be here?" Our typical response is that the career development process should be treated comprehensively and holistically. Examining individuals' life experiences to discover the meaning of and relationship to work is an important component to any clinical relationship no matter the presenting problem.

Exploring an individual's career interests is akin to the exploration of personality-specific characteristics that might bode well for clients in their search for a suitable relationship, work–life balance, and needs from their parents or individuals who influence their lives. Also, it is important to recognize that the careers we choose have an effect on the environments in which our clients and their families learn and develop, generational educational opportunities, and the way we view the self.

COURSE DESCRIPTION

The Career Counseling course explores essentially two things: (a) career development theories and (b) the career decision-making process. Some courses place a special emphasis on strategies specific to school counselors or clinicians who work with children, adolescents, and teens in making career and educational decisions. Students learn the significance of the world of work in the lifestyle of individuals. Topics covered include gender and cultural/ethnicity issues that may affect career development, strategies for career exploration, the relationship between one's career development and other life roles, career-related assessment, and technical and college career tracks of curriculum development.

COURSE OBJECTIVES

The objective of this course for students who will serve as school counselors or clinical mental health counselors is to understand the contemporary reality of the world of work. Work/career choices can determine how one's life will be lived, an individual's social network, living situation and environment, and the values and attitudes of themselves and their families. There are three course objectives that are essential to the fabric of this course: (a) students will be able to identify career development theories and decision-making models; (b) students will understand the roles, functions, and settings of contemporary career counselors; and (c) students will practically demonstrate career and educational planning, placement, follow-up, and evaluation using mock clients or case study examples.

MUST-COVER TOPICS

As mentioned previously, the salient career counseling theories that should be touched on in this course are

(a) Super's life-space, life span theory, (b) Roe's personality theory of career choice, (c) Gottfredson's theory of circumscription, compromise, and self-creation, (d) Holland's theory of types and person–environment interactions, (e) Krumboltz's learning theory of career counseling, (f) Lent, Brown, and Hackett's social cognitive career theory (SCCT), and (g) Savickas's career construction theory (CCT). There are other areas of content that should be considered as well:

1. History of career counseling and development
2. Overview of how a counselor can provide career information and counseling services in a multitude of settings
3. Acknowledgment of essential books/materials/social media/websites that are available to clinicians
4. The complex nature of work and how it impacts the lives of all people, especially looking at career from a generational perspective
5. How career will be defined in the future
6. The role technology plays in career

Super's Life-Space, Life Span Theory

Super explained that the idea of career development was a complex process that required input from various sources in multiple disciplines (Super, 1990; Super, Savickas, & Super, 1996). He pulled works from different disciplines such as industrial sociology, client-centered therapy, and personal constructs to build on several key assumptions:

1. Self-characteristics and self-concepts are uniquely different for every individual.
2. Individuals may be suited for a number of career choices.
3. The concept of self evolves over time.
4. Each career requires specific traits.

5. Career development is influenced by the stage of an individual's life.
6. Career development is influenced by personality, socioeconomic status, skills, educational opportunities, needs, community, interests, values, and family.
7. Coping with career development is influenced by the individual's process of dealing with past developmental processes.

Regarding the process of career development over an individual's life span, Super (1990) explained that career development is a person's ability to encounter developmental tasks and handle them in a way that propels the person to become the type of person he or she wants to become. Super's developmental tasks are described in Table 8.1.

TABLE 8.1 Super's Developmental Tasks

Stages	Description
Growth (Childhood): Ages 4–13	Healthily moving through this stage means being aware of the influence that past and present decisions have on the future.
Exploration (Adolescence): Ages 14–24	Career preferences are solidified. Career choices are narrowed, but not solidified.
Establishment (Early Adulthood): Ages 25–45	Stabilization and advancing in one's career are the main objectives of this stage.
Maintenance (Middle Adulthood): Ages 45–65	With an ever-advancing work environment, recycling through previous experiences is a must to improve career position and situation.
Disengagement (Late Adulthood): Ages 65+	A holistic well-being approach is needed at this stage, where work output is reduced as retirement grows nearer.

Source: Data from Super, D. E. (1953). A theory of vocational development. *American Psychologist, 8*(5), 185–190. doi:10.1037/h0056046

Roe's Personality Theory of Career Choice

Anne Roe believed that the pattern of experiences that produced either satisfaction or frustration in early childhood influenced career behavior in adulthood. Roe emphasized the importance of the environment in which a child was raised, detailing three main types of child-rearing environments:

> **Emotional Concentration:** This environment ranges from parents being overly demanding to overprotective. This environment may also provide rewards for socially desirable behavior, with parents' love and approval being conditional.
> **Avoidance:** This can range from avoiding the child's physical needs to completely rejecting the child's emotional needs.
> **Acceptance:** In this environment the child's physical and psychological needs are met.

Roe also developed an occupational classification system that highlighted eight fields: (a) service, (b) business contact, (c) arts and entertainment, (d) organization, (e) general culture, (f) technology, (g) outdoors, and (h) science. Each of these items has its own description and career examples that need to be discussed and explored within the course. Another important aspect of Roe's theory is attention to the influence of the environment and a person's needs.

Gottfredson's Theory of Circumscription, Compromise, and Self-Creation

Gottfredson's theory was developed in part to address questions such as "Why do children seem to re-create the social inequalities of their elders long before they themselves experience any barriers to pursuing their dreams?" (Gottfredson, 2002, p. 85). Gottfredson (2002) explained that an individual's career can be differentiated by three aspects: (a) masculinity–femininity, (b) occupational prestige, and (c) field of work. These aspects play an important role in how an individual perceives his or her *fit* into his or her environment. Gottfredson (2002) expressed that career satisfaction depends on whether or not an individual's career choice "allows one to implement a desired social self, either through the work itself or the lifestyle it allows self and family" (p. 107). When individuals begin to eliminate career alternatives that may be undesirable based on the three points defined here, Gottfredson described this as "circumscription." The circumscription process is composed of four stages of cognitive development:

1. Orientation to Size and Power (begin at ages 3–5): Children begin to use simple terms to classify people and orient themselves to differences in size.
2. Orientation to Sex Roles (ages 6–8): There is an awareness of sex roles, which drives career aspirations.
3. Orientation to Social Valuation (ages 9–13): Social class and prestige enter the child's awareness. Social standing and ability drive career aspiration.
4. Orientation to the Internal, Unique Self (starts at age 14): Self-awareness generates career aspirations. More congruent options are chosen (Gottfredson, 2002).

Holland's Theory of Types and Person–Environment Interactions

Holland (1973) discussed several basic assumptions to his theory. One of the most important to explore in the progression of this course is that individuals can be categorized as one of six different types and there are six kinds of environments: realistic, investigative, artistic, social, enterprising, or conventional (RIASEC). Table 8.2 describes these six types.

TABLE 8.2 Holland's Theory of Types and Person–Environment Interactions

Personality Type	Activities	Description
The realistic type	Organization of tools, objects, or machines. Jobs include farmers, electricians, or mechanics.	Conforming, materialistic, genuine, practical, shy, honest
The investigative type	Investigation of phenomena. Jobs include geologists, physicists, or chemists.	Analytical, independent, intellectual, pessimistic, introverted, critical, rational, and curious
The artistic type	Freedom and ambiguity. Jobs include musicians, actors/actresses, or designers.	Imaginative, introspective, disorderly, emotional, impulsive, nonconforming, independent, and original
The social type	Prefer to spend time around others. Jobs include teachers, counselors, or psychologists.	Convincing, cooperative, sympathetic, patient, tactful, responsible, understanding, and warm
The enterprising type	Prefer activities that entail economic gain. Job preferences include managers or entrepreneurs.	Domineering, adventurous, pleasure seeking, agreeable, ambitious, impulsive, and popular

(continued)

TABLE 8.2 Holland's Theory of Types and Person–Environment
Interactions (*continued*)

Personality Type	Activities	Description
The conventional type	Prefer the manipulation of records or data. Jobs such as bankers, adjusters, or bookkeepers suit them.	Conforming, obedient, practical, orderly, and unimaginative

Other assumptions of the theory include:

1. Individuals try to find environments that best allow them to express their skills, abilities, attitudes, and values.
2. Personality types are environmentally and genetically based.

Krumboltz's Learning Theory of Career Counseling

Krumboltz's learning theory of career counseling is composed of two parts:

1. Social learning theory of career decision-making—identifies four factors that influence career decisions
   a. Genetic endowment and special abilities
   b. Environmental conditions and events
   c. Instrumental and associative learning experiences
   d. Task-approach skills
2. Learning theory of career counseling—details ways in which career counselors help with career decisions

a. Helps individuals learn and explore assumptions as well as develop new interests and strategies (Krumboltz, Mitchell, & Gelatt, 1976)

Lent, Brown, and Hackett's SCCT

SCCT highlights the role cognitive factors play in career development. Lent and Lopez (1996) explained that self-efficacy, beliefs, outcome expectations, and goals are all interconnected regarding SCCT. The relationship between these items shapes career interests, goals, and actions. According to Lent and Brown (1996), "higher self-efficacy and anticipated positive outcomes promote higher goals, which help to mobilize and sustain performance behavior" (p. 318). However, career development issues occur when individuals choose a career option prematurely with inaccurate self-efficacy beliefs and/or outcome expectations.

Savickas's CCT

CCT addresses several career issues:

1. States the career preferences of many different individuals
2. Highlights the unique ways individuals cope with developmental transitions
3. Attends to life themes that aid in constructing meaning in individuals' career behaviors

Savickas (2005) explained that careers are constructed by the meaning individuals place on career behavior and experiences. Career adaptability is another important aspect of CCT. Specific life transitions such as moving from graduate school to collecting clinical licensure hours require adaptability.

PERSONAL EXPERIENCE: ANGELA WEINGARTNER

Teaching Approach

This course provides an overview of career development theories, career counseling techniques, and career assessment tools. Career counseling is discussed and examined in the context of working with diverse populations across schools, community agencies, and clinical practice settings.

While this is all incredibly important, what is crucial for students is to understand that what we do today is because of our beginnings as vocational counselors. On the first day of class, I have students respond to a Wordle (a word cloud generator) with the prompt "What words do you associate with taking a career counseling course?" Some students respond with words such as "excited" or "eager"; however, most students responded with words such as "unsure," "boring," "unnecessary," or even "why do we have to take this class at all?". Now as a counselor educator who is incredibly passionate about career development and career counseling, you would think my feelings would be hurt. Actually, it is just the opposite. This is what fuels me as an educator. I want to create a transformative experience for these students in this classroom that challenges previously held biases and opens their minds and hearts to new ways of working with and alongside clients. Ultimately, I hope that students leave their career course with a better understanding of themselves and see how career counseling is not done solely in a career services center, but rather, it is discussed with every client who walks into their office, school, or clinic.

Career development courses are not as impactful if they focus solely on career theory. I utilize assignments that foster reflection and application to the students' own career journeys to help them understand how career development has manifested in their own lives. Students will more likely remember theories, assessments, and interventions they have applied to themselves and will in turn have more confidence and a better understanding of how to integrate career development with clients. I incorporate PowerPoints to deliver material while also sharing my own personal stories of how my career journey is reflected within these theories. Large and small group discussions occur throughout the class period to allow students the opportunity to critically think about the lecture material. More often than not, the class ends with an experiential activity that encourages students to either think more deeply about the material or participate in a career counseling intervention they can later incorporate into their own counseling to use with future clients. To supplement learning outside of the classroom, I create assignments that require the students to reflect on their own career development and apply two or three theories to their career journey. Students report remembering theories they used in conceptualizing their own career development at a much higher rate compared to theories that were discussed only in the classroom.

To help bring diverse perspectives to career development and counseling, I invite at least three different guest speakers throughout the semester. I always have our university's Career Services department come and speak about what the center has to offer, the diverse body of students they serve, and how their career journeys led them to this position. Most of the Career Services staff have their master's degree in clinical counseling and can speak to how they use their counseling skills in a career center. I also have a guest speaker who specializes in working with the LGBTQ community come in and discuss his or her advocacy work fighting against issues related to discrimination and prejudice. It is critical that racism, discrimination, prejudice and any other form of oppression are examined in a career development course. I find that hearing from professionals who are out in the field, advocating for others, is a powerful transformative experience for graduate students.

Course Preparation

I teach this course in the fall, so I generally start course preparation in the middle of the summer. I make sure to update any recommended articles that I include in the syllabus as well as integrate new theories or techniques into the PowerPoint lectures for the semester. As counselor educators, it is essential that we are informed on the latest research and what other educators are doing in the classroom. Attending the National Career Development Association (NCDA) conference every summer is always inspirational, and I leave with new ideas on how to create a meaningful career development course. It is due to attending a presentation at NCDA that led me to create the assignment that students report enjoying the most: the Assessment Reflection Paper.

Over a 5-week time period, about halfway through the semester, I have students complete the Myers–Briggs Type Indicator (MBTI), Clifton StrengthsFinder, and the Strong Interest Inventory. Students enjoy getting to take the assessment firsthand, experience receiving their results, and understand how to apply these results to their everyday lives. It provides a well-rounded perspective of their personalities, strengths, interests, and values and how these intersect at work and at home. Students are then asked to write a reflection paper that addresses what new insights they learned about themselves, what assessment was most and least valuable, how these results will impact their future professions, and finally how they see themselves using these assessments with clients. Graduate students have shared that they value the act of taking the assessments and enjoy furthering their own self-awareness and understanding.

Advice

Teaching the career development course is my favorite course to teach. Students come in with a preconceived notion of what this class will entail, and my goal is to have them finishing the semester excited about career counseling and how they can use it with every client or student with whom they meet. The students can apply the majority of what they learn in class to their own lives and through that experience build understanding for career challenges many clients face. If this is your first time teaching this course, here are my top five tips:

1. *Create assignments that encourage student reflection.* This may seem like a no-brainer, but time and time again students tell me what they remember most are the concepts that they applied to their own career journey.
2. *Get outside the classroom.* Career development serves as a conduit to find meaning and recognize opportunities for vocational fulfillment. While some of us have found that meaning in higher education and counseling, others find meaning in seeing their crops grow, working as nurses, or building homes. Exposing students to individuals in a variety of workforce populations (single-career worker, minimum wage worker, military transition, re-entry worker, etc.) invites discussion for examining our own career biases and finding potential gaps within career services in our community.
3. *Familiarize yourself with NCDA.* The website has a number of wonderful resources for counselors, and if you are a member, you get access to *Career Convergence*, a monthly web magazine with articles specifically for counselor educators and researchers. If you can, attend the conference

and see what other career professionals are researching and discussing.

4. *Teach beyond traditional career theories.* Yes, I understand that these theories are the foundation of vocational counseling and are important to teach, and what we are seeing today in modern career counseling are theories that meet the needs of today's clients and go beyond traditional linear career paths. Educate yourself on postmodern theories and highlight how they address the needs of today's global population.

5. *Be excited.* More often than not, the career course is given to the new faculty member because no one else wants to teach it. If you are not passionate about the class, the students will not be either!

COURSE CONSIDERATIONS

Additional Textbooks

- *Career Counseling: A Holistic Approach*, by Vernon G. Zunker (2015)
- *Career Counseling: Foundations, Perspectives, and Applications*, by David Capuzzi and Mark Stauffer (2018)
- *Career Counseling: Holism, Diversity, and Strengths*, by Norman C. Gysbers, Mary J. Heppner, and Joseph A. Johnston (2014)
- *Applying Career Development Theory to Counseling*, by Richard S. Sharf (2013)

Mock Schedule

A potential course schedule may look like the example in Exhibit 8.1.

EXHIBIT 8.1 Career Counseling Course: Mock Schedule

Date	Discussion Topic	Chapter Readings	Assignments and Test Dates
Aug 20	Group Cohesion Activity		
Aug 27	Course Introductions and Syllabus Review		-Define *career*. -Messages from your family about career. -Who needs career counseling?
Sep 3	Super's Life-Space, Life Span Theory	Check Moodle for assigned reading materials	
Sep 10	Super's Life-Space, Life Span Theory	Check Moodle for assigned reading materials	
Sep 17	Roe's Personality Theory of Career Choice	Check Moodle for assigned reading materials	
Sep 24	Roe's Personality Theory of Career Choice	Check Moodle for assigned reading materials	
Oct 1	Gottfredson's Theory of Circumscription, Compromise, and Self-Creation	Check Moodle for assigned reading materials	

(continued)

EXHIBIT 8.1 Career Counseling Course: Mock Schedule (*continued*)

Date	Discussion Topic	Chapter Readings	Assignments and Test Dates
Oct 8	Gottfredson's Theory of Circumscription, Compromise, and Self-Creation	Check Moodle for assigned reading materials	
Oct 15	Holland's Theory of Types and Person–Environment Interactions	Check Moodle for assigned reading materials	Career Assessment
Oct 22	Jung Typology Assessment	Check Moodle for assigned reading materials	Career Assessment
Oct 29	Krumboltz's Learning Theory of Career Counseling	Check Moodle for assigned reading materials	
Nov 5	Krumboltz's Learning Theory of Career Counseling	Check Moodle for assigned reading materials	
Nov 12	Lent, Brown, and Hackett's Social Cognitive Career Theory	Check Moodle for assigned reading materials	
Nov 19	Savickas's Career Construction Theory	Check Moodle for assigned reading materials	

(*continued*)

EXHIBIT 8.1 Career Counseling Course: Mock Schedule (*continued*)

Date	Discussion Topic	Chapter Readings	Assignments and Test Dates
Nov 26	Assignment Presentation		
Dec 3	Course Wrap-Up		

COURSE ASSIGNMENT

Career Theory Self-Assessment

Students will use two career counseling theories to explain their career decision-making and career goals. This paper will focus on why students chose a career in the counseling field from two different career theories. Students will then compare and contrast the theories, highlighting how similar and different they are in regard to their own decision-making. The paper should be a thorough application of each theory, as well as a thorough explanation of how the theories compare and contrast in explaining their career decision-making and career goals. Throughout the paper, students should address the following:

- Which theory does a better job of explaining you and your career decision-making?
- Which would you be more likely to use with clients, and why?
- Are there any sociocultural concerns you became aware of when applying the theories to yourself, or could there be an issue when applied to someone different from you?

Your self-assessment should reflect a *critical* analysis of the applied theory. The paper should be at least five pages and follow American Psychological Association (APA) Style.

REFERENCES

Gottfredson, L. S. (2002). Gottfredson's theory of circumscription, compromise, and self-creation. In D. Brown & Associates (Eds.), *Career choice and development* (4th ed., pp. 85–148). San Francisco, CA: Jossey-Bass.

Holland, J. L. (1973). *Making vocational choices: A theory of careers.* Upper Saddle River, NJ: Prentice Hall.

Lent, E. B., & Lopez, F. G. (1996). Congruence from many angles: Relations of multiple congruence indices to job satisfaction among adult workers. *Journal of Vocational Behavior, 49*, 24–37. doi:10.1006/jvbe.1996.0031

Lent, R. W., & Brown, S. D. (1996). Social cognitive approach to career development: An overview. *The Career Development Quarterly, 44*, 310–321. doi:10.1002/j.2161-0045.1996.tb00448.x

Savickas, M. L. (2005). The theory and practice of career construction. In S. D. Brown & R. W. Lent (Eds.), *Career development and counseling* (pp. 42–70). Hoboken, NJ: Wiley.

Super, D. E. (1953). A theory of vocational development. *American Psychologist, 8*(5), 185–190. doi:10.1037/h0056046

Super, D. E. (1990). A life-span, life-space approach to career development. In D. Brown, L. Brooks, & Associates (Eds.), *Career choice and development: Applying contemporary theories to practice* (2nd ed.). San Francisco, CA: Jossey-Bass.

Super, D. E., Savickas, M. L., & Super, C. M. (1996). The life-span, life-space approach to careers. In D. Brown, L. Brooks, & Associates (Eds.), *Career choice development: Applying contemporary theories to practice* (3d ed., pp. 121–178). San Francisco, CA: Jossey-Bass.

FURTHER READING

Bandura, A. (1986). *Social foundations of thought and action: A social-cognitive theory*. Upper Saddle River, NJ: Prentice Hall.

Buehler, C. (1933). *Der menschliche lebenslauf als psychologisches problem*. Leipzig, Germany: Hirzel.

Gottfredson, L. S. (1996). A theory of circumscription and compromise. In D. Brown, L. Brooks, & Associates (Eds.), *Career choice and development* (3rd ed., pp. 179–281). San Francisco, CA: Jossey-Bass.

Gottfredson, L. S. (2003). The challenge and promise of cognitive career assessment. *Journal of Career Assessment*, 11, 115–135. doi:10.1177/1069072703011002001

Havighurst, R. J. (1951). Validity of the Chicago Attitude Inventory as a measure of personal adjustment in old age. *Journal of Abnormal and Social Psychology, 46*(1), 24–29. doi:10.1037/h0057629

Havighurst, R. J. (1953). *Human development and education*. New York, NY: Longmans Green.

Holland, J. L. (1959). A theory of vocational choice. *Journal of Counseling Psychology, 6*, 35–45. doi:10.1037/h0040767

Kelly, G. A. (1955). *The psychology of personal constructs*. New York, NY: W. W. Norton.

Krumboltz, J. D., Mitchell, A., & Gelatt, H. G. (1976). Applications of social learning theory of career selection. *Focus on Guidance, 8*, 71–81. Retrieved from https://doi.org/10.1177/001100007600600117

Lent, R. W. (2013). Career-life preparedness: Revisiting career planning and adjustment in the new workplace. *The Career Development Quarterly, 61*, 2–14. doi:10.1002/j.2161-0045.2013.00031.x

Miller, D. C., & Form, W. H. (1951). *Industrial sociology*. New York, NY: Harper & Row.

Rogers, C. R. (1951). Client-centered therapy, its current practice, implications, and theory. Boston, MA: Houghton Mifflin.

Savickas, M. L. (2013). Career construction theory and practice. In S. D. Brown & R. W. Lent (Eds.), *Career development and counseling* (2nd ed., pp. 147–186). Hoboken, NJ: Wiley.

Super, D. E. (1951). Vocational adjustment: Implementing a self-concept. *Occupations, 51*, 88–92. doi:10.1002/j.2164-5892.1951.tb02607.x

Super, D. E. (1976). *Career education and the meaning of work.* Washington, DC: Office of Education.

Super, D. E. (1980). A life-span, life-space approach to career development. *Journal of Vocational Behavior, 16*, 282–298. doi:10.1016/0001-8791(80)90056-1

9 GROUP COUNSELING COURSES

INTRODUCTION

The effort involved in constructing this course is considerable, yet this course is essential for students' understanding of holding multiple processes and understanding
process and content components of the therapeutic process. Typically, this course can be a source of fear and anxiety for students. As one of our students put it, "I am just
trying to learn to be in the room with just one person.
Now you are telling me there will be multiple people in
there with me!" Group counseling can provide a powerful place for growth and healing, which can be intimidating for some students. In constructing this course, there is
always a parallel process that happens—as you teach the
inner workings of the group counseling process, a quasi-
group counseling process is happening in the moment
with students in the class. It is important to pay attention
to and use the class's process as an instrument of learning.

COURSE DESCRIPTION

The group counseling course covers the group development process, dynamics of the therapeutic relationship,
and theories and techniques of group counseling. In addition to these topics, the course explores leadership styles,

roles of group members, ethical and legal issues related to group interventions, as well as the various types of groups. This course is essentially designed to facilitate students' examination of the different stages in group development, the implications of different approaches to conducting groups for diverse populations, and exploring the role in creating a group process and culture.

COURSE OBJECTIVES

Upon completion of this course, students will demonstrate understanding of the following:

1. Group process components, group members' roles and behaviors, developmental stage theories, and relational factors of group work
2. Characteristics of various types of group leaders and leadership styles
3. Theories of group counseling
4. Methods of group counseling, including counselor orientations and behaviors
5. Group member selection methods
6. Methods of evaluation of effectiveness
7. Types of group work, including task groups, psychoeducational groups, and therapy groups
8. Ethical and legal considerations related to group work
9. Their own personal biases and growth areas through participation as a group member

MUST-COVER TOPICS

Types of Groups

At the onset of the class, it is important to discuss the different type of groups students may have the opportunity to lead in the field. The specific groups that students may have the opportunity to lead are as follows:

1. **Task groups:** The main focus of these groups is to apply principles and processes of the group to enhance practice of recognized work goals. Example of groups such as these are task force groups that have a clear goal toward which the group is working, perhaps improving patient comfort and hospitality services with patient family members.

2. **Psychoeducational groups:** Targeted education for members is the focus of this group. An example would be a parent–child relational group where members are educated on how to create healthy relationships with their children.

3. **Counseling groups:** These groups highlight the interpersonal process and problem-solving strategies of group members. They also help members explore and communicate their thoughts, feelings, and behaviors.

4. **Psychotherapy groups:** The focus is on remediating psychological problems and interpersonal problems of living for individual group members. Group members may present with issues that are suggestive of acute or chronic distress or impairment in functioning.

5. **Brief groups:** These are groups that are time limited.

Common Issues Facing Beginning Group Leaders

Becoming a culturally skilled group counselor is one of the most salient issues for students today. Diversity and cultural issues are important because as the world becomes increasingly diverse, so do the clients with whom students work. And by and large, so do the types of groups that students will lead. It is important to explore the impact of cultural factors that are at play within the group as well as each client's life. It is also just as important for students to acquire understanding of their own cultural conditioning and awareness of the sociopolitical system to which they belong.

Other important issues facing beginning group leaders can be illuminated through the common questions that have been asked throughout our time teaching this course:

1. "I mean, how do I even start the group?":
   A common issue for beginning group leaders is not only knowing how to start the group but being specifically aware of what words to say when starting a group.
2. "Should I make sure that I respond to all of the group members?": Students can feel pressure and anxiety to make sure that each group member feels heard and understood. It may be important to mention the importance of understanding process and content and how a group process can be influenced by the leader's attempt to respond to every statement made.
3. "What if I don't like one of the group members?": This question is one of the most important issues in this course because it highlights the student need to understand and explore what it would be like to enter into a therapeutic relationship with multiple people where their feelings toward a specific client can influence the group dynamic.
4. "Have you ever made a mistake? What did you do?": Being transparent about the difficulty of leading a group is an important normalizer for students. At times, hearing that mistakes are an inevitable part of the process helps students cope

with a truth that is a part of the work
we do.

5. "How rigid should my group rules be? Like,
   should I interrupt members who break rules?":
   A common issue for students going into group
   is the unpredictability of having multiple people
   in the room at one time. This issue could cause
   some students to be anxious about controlling
   group members or policing the process. It is
   important to share with students the many
   different ways that group leaders and groups as
   a whole create and enforce group rules.

6. "Should I share my personal life if the group
   brings up a topic I am close to?": The self-
   disclosure question is not unique to this course,
   but it is uniquely answered by professors of this
   course. An important question to explore is what
   students may or may not be comfortable sharing
   and also how self-disclosing may affect group
   dynamics.

7. "What if a group member does not like me?":
   The bigger question here is what would it be
   like for you to not be liked by a group member.
   Would it shift how you behave or what you
   think of that individual? These questions are
   important because they affect the way students
   view group relational process with regard to
   group work.

Ethical and Legal Issues in Group Counseling

Essentially, there are three important types of ethical
issues; (a) legal issues, (b) clinical issues, and (c) cultural issues. Legal issues can be defined as the enforce-
able standards that society will tolerate. Clinical issues
highlight a clinician using his or her own judgment to
stay in accordance with legal mandates. Other ethical and

legal issues that may be of benefit for students to explore are:

1. A group leader's use of power
2. A group leader's propensity to self-disclose and awareness of the reasons behind disclosing
3. Issues surrounding confidentiality from the group leader and members
4. Group members' ability to scapegoat or gaslight and the leader's response to these tactics
5. Issues surrounding confrontation and what that looks like for the student within the group setting

Theories and Techniques of Group Counseling

It is important for students to grapple with the role that theory has in facilitating a group. It guides the way students are within relationships and helps to solidify the students' roles within a group. Techniques help to prompt movement within a group. Anything a group leader does within the group is a technique. Techniques could range from experimenting with new behaviors to staying completely silent. In communicating theories to students as a brief refresher for some students who may have already taken the theories course, theories can be broken down into four categories:

1. *Psychodynamic approaches* include psychoanalytic and Adlerian therapy.
2. *Experiential approaches* include existential, person-centered, and Gestalt therapy.
3. *Cognitive behavioral approaches* include behavior, cognitive, rational emotive behavior, and reality therapies.
4. *Postmodern approaches* include solution-focused brief therapy, narrative therapy, and feminist therapy.

Stages of Development in the Group Process

Initial Stage
This stage is marked by the orientation process of the group. Group members have the propensity to present a more socially acceptable side to themselves, which means that new group leaders need to be patient while this very normal part of the process takes place. There is a delicate balance within this stage where individuals may feel anxious and/or insecure about expressing themselves fully without any group structure. Group structure helps by giving members insight into how to treat the group process and each other. This structure may include creating group norms, rules, and expectations.

Transition Stage
During this stage, members begin to start working on the issues that prompted their need to join the group in the first place. Similar to the initial stage, the balancing act that members play is the risk of being vulnerable with individuals whom they may not know. It is important for group leaders to process anxiety surrounding sharing and potentially feeling like they are being judged.

Working Stage
This stage is marked by the specific depth of the work that group members do. Group members tend to share in an open, honest, and vulnerable manner. For new group leaders, it may be important to explore their fears or hesitations regarding members' vulnerability and their ability to cultivate that safe environment that allows for good group work to be done.

Final Stage
This stage allows for members to slow down the process and explore what was learned throughout the group therapy process. Group leaders should attend to the

members' feelings regarding terminating the group and how they will keep themselves safe as the group process ends. It is also important for students to explore their feelings toward ending what could be a powerful clinical experience for them.

PERSONAL EXPERIENCE

Teaching Approach

This course has a lot of moving parts. On the one hand, students are coping with the fact that they will be working with multiple individuals in the room, which can be anxiety producing. On the other hand, students are synthesizing the counseling theories that they have learned and trying to make them make sense within the group therapy setting. Our approach in this course is to be genuine about our experience running groups and trying to humanize their fears or hesitations with this type of therapy. We use a combination of real-life group participation, mock group therapy scenarios in class, and witnessing other well-respected group therapists in the field do group therapy through the medium of videos. This approach allows for in-depth discussion about students' experiences participating in a group outside of class, but also this group participation gives students the *group member insight*, which informs their decisions as clinicians.

Student Experience

This course resonates with students because there is so much vulnerability within the act of sharing the therapeutic process with other individuals. Because of the powerful nature of group therapy, students may appear timid regarding course material or in-class activities. Unlike other courses, the group therapy learning process is high paced—students are performing multiple tasks while trying to keep track of their own experiences that may influence the group. Also, the group therapy process prompts students to deal with their own fears of rejection from the group, needs to be liked or respected by group members, as well as their ability to handle the ambiguous nature of group stages.

Course Preparation

In preparing for this course, there is a significant question that usually needs to be answered: How are the students going to gain suitable, healthy, and educational group member experience? One way in which we have tried to answer this question is to run several mock therapy groups throughout the course of the semester with us being the leader and the students being the members. We have had doctoral-level clinicians lead the group. We also had clinicians or alumni come back to the university to voluntarily run the group process for students. To answer this question, educators should take into account (a) the dual role that students will have to play as a peer and also a group member, (b) confidentiality issues and student hesitancy to be vulnerable if their professor is also their group leader, and (c) the dual relationships that might exist with alumni or outside clinicians if those individuals decided to run a group.

Nuts and Bolts

Plan to answer a plethora of student questions regarding group dynamics as well as ethical issues that may exist within the group therapy process. Processing openly the experiences from leading other groups will give context and shed light on the information students are absorbing from the books and videos. It is also important to watch group therapy videos that allow for questions to arise and a learning opportunity to erupt while exploring an adequate answer.

COURSE CONSIDERATIONS

Additional Textbooks

The following list includes suggested textbooks used for the group therapy course:

> *Theory and Practice of Group Counseling* (9th ed.), by Gerald Corey (2016)
> *The Theory and Practice of Group Psychotherapy* (5th ed.), by Irvin D. Yalom (2005)

Mock Schedule

The mock schedule in Exhibit 9.1 was developed as if *Theory and Practice of Group Counseling* (9th ed.), by Gerald Corey (2016), was the course textbook.

COURSE ASSIGNMENTS

The following are examples of course assignments counselor educators can use when preparing to teach the group therapy course.

Group Theory Papers

Students will write two 4-page body length papers (not including the title page, reference page, etc.) in American Psychological Association (APA) style on a group theory using six references not including the class textbook.

EXHIBIT 9.1 Group Counseling Course: Mock Schedule

Academic Date	Topic	Assignment	Standards
Aug 21	Overview Chapter 1*	Review of course syllabus Review of Chapter 1 Assignment: Read Chapters 2 and 3	2F6b; 2F6f; 2F6g; 2F6h
Aug 28	Chapters 2 and 3	Review of Chapters 2 and 3 Assignment: Read Chapters 4 and 5	Chapter 2: 2F6a; 2F6b; 2F6c; 2F6d Chapter 3: 2F6g; 5C2a; 5C2j; 5C2k; 5C2l
Sep 4		Review of Chapters 3 and 4	
Sep 11	Chapters 4 and 5	Review of Chapters 4 and 5 Assignment: Read Chapter 6	Chapter 4: 2F6b; 2F6e Chapter 5: 2F6b; 2F6c; 2F6f
Sep 18	Chapter 6	Review of Chapter 6 Facilitation: Psychoanalytic Therapy Assignment: Read Chapter 7	2F6a; 2F6b; 2F6c; 2F6h; 5C2j
Sep 25	Chapter 7	Review of Chapter 7 Facilitation: Adlerian Therapy Assignment: Read Chapter 8	2F6a; 2F6b; 2F6c; 2F6h; 5C2j

(continued)

EXHIBIT 9.1 Group Counseling Course: Mock Schedule (*continued*)

Academic Date	Topic	Assignment	Standards
Oct 2	Chapter 8	Review of Chapter 8 Facilitation: Psychodrama	2F6a; 2F6b; 2F6c; 2F6h; 5C2j
Oct 9	Chapter 9	Review of Chapter 9 Facilitation: Gestalt Therapy	
Oct 16	Chapter 10	Facilitation: Existential Therapy Review of Chapter 10	2F6a; 2F6b; 2F6c; 2F6d; 2F6e; 2F6f; 2F6g; 5C2a; 5C2j; 5C2k; 5C2l
Oct 23	Chapter 11	Review of Chapter 11 Facilitation: Person-Centered Therapy	2F6a; 2F6b; 2F6c; 2F6h; 5C2j
Oct 30		*Due: Group Field Experience*	2F6a; 2F6b; 2F6c; 2F6h; 5C2j
Nov 6		Group facilitation	2F6a; 2F6b; 2F6c; 2F6h; 5C2j
Nov 13		Group facilitation	2F6a; 2F6b; 2F6c; 2F6h; 5C2j
Nov 19		Group facilitation	2F6a; 2F6b; 2F6c; 2F6h; 5C2j
Nov 26		Group facilitation	2F6a; 2F6b; 2F6c; 5C2j

*Listed chapter topics and readings refer to Corey, G. (2016). *Theory and practice of group counseling* (9th ed.). Boston, MA: Cengage Learning.

Students may pick from any of the following subjects for each of the papers:

- Groups for children
- Groups for adolescents
- Groups for grief
- Groups for individuals of color
- Groups for the LGBTQ community
- Psychoanalytic/psychodynamic
- Adlerian groups
- Person-centered groups
- Existential groups
- Gestalt groups
- Rational emotive behavior therapy (REBT) groups
- Behavioral therapy groups
- Reality therapy groups
- Cognitive behavioral therapy groups
- Others as approved by your professor

Group Facilitation

Each student will participate in a 30-minute process group facilitation during class time and submit an individualized written paper (two to four pages) on the topic used in the group. Facilitation and paper must include the following:

a. Comprehensive summary of the topic in terms of breadth and depth of material presented
b. Report of experience running the group: (a) areas of growth, (b) areas that went well, (c) any changes they would have made
c. An activity involving all of the group members
d. Submission of the paper by 6:00 p.m. on the date of assigned oral presentation

Group Field Experience

Students will participate in at least three group field experiences within the community and submit proof of participation. Students will verbally present to the class their experiences in their chosen group experience in a 30-minute presentation. The presentation should indicate the type of group the student attended, the student's personal experience being a group member, and any tenets from the text/class lectures highlighted during the time in the group experience.

10 | RESEARCH COURSES

INTRODUCTION

The dreaded research course is often the source of many students' fears when starting the graduate program. The goal of this course is to introduce students to the basic concepts and techniques of research used in the counseling profession. The course is designed to be theoretical and applied. Students will develop an understanding of basic qualitative and quantitative research design and basic statistical analysis. An important phrase in this course's description is the word "basic." Some counselor educators forget that this course is not an advanced statistics course for students looking forward to becoming statisticians. These counselor educators are overly excited about diving into Statistical Package for Social Sciences (SPSS) and NVivo with students and calculating standard deviations by hand. While this excitement is admirable, it can cause these counselor educators to lose sight of their students' needs and those students' real-life relationships to research after graduation. See Dukic (2015) to better understand the research training environment and its potential influence on graduate level counseling students' attitudes toward and interest in research. According to Rodriguez and Toews (2005), these research courses focus on conducting a research study and not how to evaluate how research informs practice. Students are expected to learn evaluation skills through the process of formulating a research study (Rodriguez & Toews, 2005). According to Reisetter et al.

(2004), when courses are taught this way, students may not understand the connection between research findings and clinical application. Additionally, because these types of research courses do not focus on helping clients directly, students become disengaged from research.

COURSE DESCRIPTION

Essentially, counselor educators are training students to bridge the gap between research and practice. Ideally, if students see the utility of research in their professional lives, then they may be more interested in conducting, reading, and understanding research. So this course needs to be useful. Counselor educators need to be intentional about any research-related topic or idea that cannot be directly related to students' work with clients. Students in internship need to be able to read an article and use the findings in their next session. So, this course gives students the tools to be able to find research articles, break them down, and pull out essential information that will enhance their clinical work. During this process, students will grasp a basic understanding of statistical concepts and the steps to conduct qualitative and quantitative research studies. This course is important because it trains students on how to build their competence.

COURSE OBJECTIVES

Here is a scenario in which this course is most beneficial to students: A student attends a therapy session and identifies a clinical issue to which he or she needs support to address. That student then leaves the session, seeks supervision, and consults the extant literature regarding the clinical issue. While reading relevant and current literature, the student is able to identify and understand the researchers' methodology, strengths and limitations, research findings, discussion, and implications for his or her clinical issue. The student can then use this knowledge to inform his or her clinical work. Students will walk away from this course with the ability to understand and evaluate the qualitative and quantitative research of others. They will engage in discussion regarding what should constitute as quality research. Students will become familiar with and use qualitative and quantitative terminology. They will comprehend the basic tenets of the main social science theories as related to qualitative and quantitative research. Students will be exposed to an array of possible methods, analyses, and ways of representing and writing up qualitative and quantitative research. They will design original research with the option to conduct this study. Students will understand and utilize methods to enhance trustworthiness, reliability, and validity of a study. Students will appreciate the code of ethics necessary when conducting research. Finally, they will become familiar with the Institutional Review Board (IRB) human subjects process.

MUST-COVER TOPICS

The following sections briefly describe some of the must-cover topics in this course. These topics are not all that is covered in this course. For example, staples of this course include topics such as coding qualitative data, independent and dependent variables, measures of central tendency, and analyzing data. Most research books make these topics unavoidable when preparing for this course. The topics here include some common ones and also some that may not be obvious but can be helpful when covered.

Philosophical Foundations of Human Behavior

According to Creswell and Poth (2017), writers about research focus on four philosophies that affect the methods researchers use to conduct research studies. This course focuses on four foundational philosophies: positivism, postpositivism, constructivism, and critical theory. *Positivism* holds the ideas that truth exists and there is a real reality that can be known. Researchers from this perspective remain objective throughout the process. They are not affected by the research, nor does the research affect them. *Postpositivism* also ascribes to the idea that there is a real reality; however, from this perspective, truth can never be fully known. Postpositivist researchers have biases that can affect their work, and they believe that there are flaws within all research. *Constructivism* is a perspective that suggests there is no real reality or truth. Instead, truth is developed within the minds of others. Constructivist researchers believe that each individual constructs his or her own reality and this reality can be understood only when the researcher interacts with the participants. *Critical theory* is similar to constructivism, except, however, where constructivists view individuals as constructing reality, critical theorists believe reality is shaped by forces such as society, culture, history, politics, and economics. Critical theory researchers understand that their values significantly influence their work. The findings are filtered through the researcher's interpretations that are influenced by their values and the relationship between them and the participants. These four philosophies guide students' perspectives regarding the way research is to be conducted (Creswell & Poth, 2017).

The Scientist-Practitioner Model

As Nystul (2015) explained, counselors have both an artistic and scientific aspect of their work with clients. The scientific-practitioner model captures the interdependence of these two aspects of counseling. Within the *scientific* perspective, students learn about research design and the philosophies that influence these designs. They know how to apply statistics and use clinical assessments, as well as being abreast of current literature. From the *practical* perspective, students are involved in clinical work. They understand how to apply counseling models and theories to their work. This course has to balance these perspectives within each student.

Evidence-Based Practice

This is a term that is tossed around throughout students' matriculation in their program. Some students struggle to understand what it means and how it applies to their work. According to Sommers-Flanagan (2015), evidence-based practice is therapy based on peer-reviewed scientific evidence. The aim of evidence-based practice is to provide quality treatment and accountability so that clients receive proven treatments. It is important for students to be trained as researchers as well as practitioners so that they can consume literature that informs their practice. Without a basic understanding of research and its application to their work, it would be difficult for clinicians to use evidence-based practices.

Ethics in Counseling Research

Many of the topics discussed in this section of the course may have been covered in the ethics courses. Students may have taken that course early in their program. It is important to remind students of how ethics applies to research. Counselor educators might decide to cover ethical principles such as nonmaleficence, beneficence, autonomy, justice, fidelity, or veracity, along with ethical issues related to scholarly work such as honesty and integrity. Other topics in this area to cover in this course include reporting the results, plagiarism, participants, informed consent, deception, confidentiality, debriefing, and publication credit or authorship.

Major Designs

Qualitative Designs. Qualitative research has five main methods to cover in this course: ethnography, narrative, phenomenology, grounded theory, and the case study. In an *ethnographic* study, researchers immerse themselves in the culture of their participants. They attempt to understand their culture, difficulties, and drives. Ethnographic researchers collect data through observations and interviews. The *narrative* approach focuses on individuals' lives as told through their stories. The *phenomenological* design aims to capture the lived experience of the participants. For example, phenomenological researchers might study the lived experience of single mothers in graduate school. The *grounded theory* approach tries to explain the process of an activity or event, for example, how to start a counseling private practice. *Case study* research involves examining a bounded system and developing a deep understanding using many different types of data sources.

Quantitative Designs. There are four main types of quantitative research designs to cover in this course: descriptive, correlational, quasi-experimental, and experimental. *Descriptive* designs aims to describe what is, or the current status of a variable. Data collection is typically observable. An example study would be a description of adults' attitudes toward soccer. A *correlational* design examines the relationship between variables. However, it does not determine causation. An example is the study of the relationship between graduate record examination (GRE) scores and clinical effectiveness. The *quasi-experimental* design does attempt to establish cause and effect. In this design, researchers do not assign participants to a control group or experimental group, nor do they manipulate the independent variable. An example would be the study of the effect of an after-school activity on adolescent grade point average (GPA). The *experimental* design, or true experiment, establishes cause-and-effect relationships between two or more variables. This design attempts to control for all variables when manipulating the independent variable. An example of an experiment is the study of CrossFit on blood pressure levels of African Americans.

Literature Review

A literature review is a critical examination, discussion, and summary of the extant literature regarding a specific topic. The ability to conduct an in-depth literature review is important to students' work with clients. The challenge is making students understand this fact. From a researcher's perspective, the literature review can show how proposed research is related to previous research. It also shows the relevance of a research problem. The literature review can also justify the chosen methodology. From a practitioner's perspective, being able to conduct a critical literature review can support clients' treatments. It can provide answers for clients that may spark their change in therapy. There is not one specific way to conduct a literature review, but students need to be walked through the process from finding articles, critiquing them, to summarizing the findings for clients.

PERSONAL EXPERIENCE

The following sections focus on our experience teaching the research courses. Again, our discussions are *a* way to teach these courses, not *the* way to teach them. Our hope is that readers use our experience to better prepare their courses.

Teaching Approach

As students, we took a research course before we knew we would apply for a doctoral degree. While in that course we did lose interest in research because we could not connect it to our work with clients. Now, as counselor educators, we know that there are students like us in class struggling to understand the skewness of a bell-shaped curve and wondering about its importance. So, our approach to teaching this research course is painfully practical. We want to drive home the connection between research and practice.

The course is split in thirds. The first third of the course focuses on the philosophical, ethical, and professional issues in research. The second third focuses on qualitative methods. The last third focuses on quantitative methods. Each class includes a PowerPoint lecture, a clinical case examination, critique of relevant literature using a specific method and articles related to the case, and then a class discussion and formation of a research study that might serve the case's specific population. The idea is to get students to use research to serve their clients. Then this approach helps students see how their clients could benefit from a research study.

Student Experience

When taught this way, some students tend to be less intimidated by the research aspect of the course. Learning how to conduct a research study is a by-product of their ability to critically review literature from multiple methods that are all related to clinical cases. Applying the research methods and discussions to their sessions with clients engages students in the research process. Other students might be disappointed in the lack of difficult statistical topics covered in this course. These students may plan to join a doctoral program upon graduation and feel underprepared. However, students who plan to begin a doctoral program will have all of the basic knowledge to build upon from a research course that is taught practically.

Course Preparation

This course takes quite a bit of preparation. If the course was scheduled to meet on Thursday and today was Monday, we would start preparing for this course on Monday. The topics discussed in each class are complex. It is important to explain them in a way that students can not only receive but also put into practice during their upcoming sessions. We begin by prepping the PowerPoint lecture presentation for the week. For example, if the week's class topic was phenomenology, we would prepare a lecture covering this method in depth. We would then move onto the case presentation focusing on a population that lends itself to this research method. For example, we may choose the client to be a military wife whose husband was just deployed. We believe this case may give students more opportunities to find and critique articles, as well as develop phenomenological research inspired by this case. After the case is developed and the lecture is complete, we do a cursory search for related literature. We will allow students to split up into groups during class and do a detailed search for articles. To help students formulate their own research study, we will use a predeveloped set of questions. Students will use their knowledge of the current research to process their next steps in session with the case, as well as future phenomenology research studies related to the case.

The challenge of this course is familiarizing students with the process of the course. Students may struggle to understand what they are supposed to do during the first couple of class meetings. This may frustrate students and cause them not to buy into the process. Once students are able to settle into the process, they may find that this process parallels how they use evidence-based practices when working with clients. This process may help bridge the gap between research and practice. Another challenge when preparing for this course is the balance between oversimplification and overcomplicating the information. Counselor educators must curate the information students will receive regarding each research method. Without this intentionality, students can become disengaged with the research process.

Nuts and Bolts

Each class period takes careful orchestrating to accomplish each task. During the class period we typically lecture on the day's method, and then we present and discuss a clinical case. Following this discussion, students are divided into groups where they will find and critique relevant literature using the day's method and focus on the issues presented in the case. Once the class does this, we will discuss gaps in the literature. Then the class will discuss and format a research study that might fill this gap and serve the case's specific population.

During each class meeting, we collect the relevant literature students found and post it on the course's online platform. Students will have access to this literature when preparing for quizzes and exams. Student will also be able to refer to this literature when developing research studies. The development of a research study is one of the most meaningful assignments in this course. After practicing as a group for the semester, students get to choose their favorite methodology and topic to develop a mock research study. Hopefully, the practice helps students become more proficient at developing research studies, which reflects in the grading of the assignment.

Advice

It is satisfying to watch students become more engaged scientific practitioners. As we mentioned earlier, most students enter this course intimidated by the concepts.

Often, their anxiety gets into the way of their ability to learn the concepts early in this course. Students begin to develop a flow in class, without thinking about how this process will mirror their evidence-based practice when seeing clients. This course does present challenges; some are outlined throughout this chapter. We do, however, have advice for counselor educators teaching this course for the first time:

- Be mindful of what students need to know leaving the course. Sometimes counselor educators teach this course as if all students will apply for doctoral degrees upon graduation.
- Roll with confusion. This class is complex and discusses topics counseling students majoring in psychology want to avoid: math. Students may tend to find it difficult to understand concepts.
- Make the class practical. Literature discussed in this chapter outlines the dangers of not connecting research to practice.
- Improve time management during class periods. Enlist the help of students to be mindful of the time during class as well.
- Develop case studies that students may see during their practicum and internship experience. This can drive home the usefulness of research in clinical practice.

COURSE CONSIDERATIONS

Additional Textbooks

The following is a list of suggested textbooks counselor educators can consider when preparing for this course:

- *Counseling Research: A Practitioner-Scholar Approach,* by Richard Balkin and David Kleist (2016)

- *Research Design in Counseling*, by Paul P. Heppner, Bruce E. Wampold, Jesse Owen, Kenneth T. Wang, and Mindi N. Thompson (2015)
- *Counseling Research: Quantitative, Qualitative, and Mixed Methods*, by Carl J. Sheperis, J. Scott Young, and M. Harry Daniels (2016)
- *Research Design: Qualitative, Quantitative, and Mixed Methods Approaches*, by John W. Creswell and J. David Creswell (2018)

Mock Schedule

Exhibit 10.1 presents a mock schedule as if *Research Design in Counseling*, by Heppner, Wampold, Owen, Wang, and Thompson (2015), was the course textbook.

EXHIBIT 10.1 Research Course: Mock Schedule

Date	Course Content
Jan 16	Course Orientation Philosophical Foundations Scientific Method
Jan 23	Ethics in Counseling Research
Jan 30	Establishing the Foundation for a Study
Feb 6	Designing a Qualitative Study
Feb 13	Phenomenology
Feb 20	Grounded Theory
Feb 27	Ethnography
Mar 6	Case Study
Mar 13 Spring Break	
Mar 20	Designing a Quantitative Study
Mar 27	Descriptive designs

(continued)

EXHIBIT 10.1 Research Course: Mock Schedule (*continued*)

Date	Course Content
Apr 3	Correlational Designs
Apr 10	Quasi-Experimental
Apr 17	Experimental Designs
Apr 24	Mixed Methods Research
May 1	Research Design Overview
May 8	Final Exam

COURSE ASSIGNMENTS

There are several experiential assignments used to enhance students' understanding of the complex concepts in this course. This section highlights a few.

Research Proposal and In-Class Presentation

The purpose of the project is to experientially expose students to all parts of research. Student groups (no more than three) will construct a mock research project and research plan. Depending upon the number of students, each student can create his or her own project or work in groups. The creation of this research study will include a research design, idea modification, literature review, methods for data collection, statistical analysis likely to be used, and how results will be reported. The research paper outline will be presented in American Psychological Association (APA) format. Students will be expected to use professional texts and peer-reviewed journal articles. (Specific instructions will be given in handout form to the class.) This project is broken down into five smaller assignments:

- Project outline
- Introducing hypothesis/research question
- Literature review outline
- Research methods
- Ethical consideration: Institutional Review Board (IRB) application

Groups will provide a short, in-class presentation (10 minutes) that will include a discussion of literature review outline, research question(s), research design, and the researcher's learning experience from this project. Handouts are required for full credit.

Interview a Professor/Researcher

Students will interview a professor in counselor education, school counseling, or other educational field via Skype, telephone, or face-to-face. This professor has to work for a different university. The professor/researcher must have a terminal degree and a minimum of five peer-reviewed publications or two published books. Students are to write a reflection paper about the issues that raised salience about research related to counseling and/or education. Students ought to be discouraged from offering a summary of the interview. This paper should be typed and double spaced, and the body of the paper should be a minimum of three pages in length. The purpose of this assignment is for students to engage in conversations about research and potentially build a mentorship relationship. Students will also understand research agendas and approaches to contributing to the field using research. Sample interview questions will be provided.

Critique and Analysis of Articles

Students will select 10 research articles from peer-refereed journals (electronic or print) related to a topic that is of interest to them and write a critical analysis of each article. For this assignment, students should not summarize what researchers found, but rather provide their own interpretation of what was done, how it was done, was it appropriate or not, and why. This paper must follow APA format and be three to five pages long. Some recommended journals include:

- *Journal of Counseling & Development (JCD)*
- *Journal of Mental Health Counseling*
- *Educational and Psychological Measurement*
- *Journal of Multicultural Counseling and Development (JMCD)*
- *Measurement and Evaluation in Counseling and Development (MECD)*
- *Professional School Counseling*
- *The Family Journal*

REFERENCES

Creswell, J. W., & Poth, C. N. (2017). *Qualitative inquiry and research design: Choosing among five approaches*. Thousand Oaks, CA: SAGE.

Dukic, M. S. (2015). The research training environment and its potential influence on graduate level counseling students' attitudes toward and interest in research. *Vistas Online Journal, 12*, 1–11. Retrieved from https://www.counseling.org/docs/default-source/vistas/the-research-training-environment-and-its-potential-influence-on-graduate-level-counseling-students-attitudes-toward-and-interest-in-research.pdf?sfvrsn=6

Nystul, M. S. (2015). *Introduction to counseling: An art and science perspective*. Thousand Oaks, CA: SAGE.

Reisetter, M., Korcuska, J. S., Yexley, M., Bonds, D., Nikels, H., & McHenry, W. (2004). Counselor educators and qualitative research: Affirming a research identity. *Counselor Education and Supervision, 44*(1), 2–16. doi:10.1002/j.1556-6978.2004.tb01856.x

Rodriguez, A., & Toews, M. L. (2005). Training students to be better consumers of research: Evaluating empirical research reports. *College Teaching, 53*(3), 99–101. doi:10.3200/CTCH.53.3.99-101

Sommers-Flanagan, J. (2015). Evidence-based relationship practice: Enhancing counselor competence. *Journal of Mental Health Counseling, 37*(2), 95–108. doi:10.17744/mehc.37.2.g13472044600588r

11 DIAGNOSIS, ASSESSMENT, AND TREATMENT PLANNING COURSES

INTRODUCTION

Most programs separate these courses into two distinct ones: Diagnosis and Treatment Planning is one course, and Assessment is another. In this chapter we cover the content as if they were separate courses. These courses go hand in hand. In fact, students often take Assessment before Diagnosis and Treatment Planning. These courses cover what typically happens in the first to third sessions of therapy. Students build rapport with clients and complete informal or formal assessments to identify the clients' problems and potential diagnoses. Then students use the gathered information and symptoms of the diagnoses to codevelop treatment plans for therapy that meet the clients' needs. The following sections cover information that can help counselor educators prepare to teach these courses for the first time.

COURSE DESCRIPTION

Diagnosis and Treatment Planning

In short, this course introduces students to the relationship between diagnosis and treatment planning. This course reviews the *Diagnostic and Statistical Manual of Mental Disorders* (5th ed.; *DSM-5*; American Psychiatric

Association, 2013) and related information regarding the diagnoses. The course focuses on the etiology of diagnoses, systemic treatment planning, and short-term and long-term interventions.

Assessment

This course introduces students to using assessment procedures in counseling. The course focuses on using basic measurement concepts as well as quantitative and qualitative assessment methods. The procedures covered in this course include observations, interviews, formal or norm-referenced assessments, and informal assessments.

COURSE OBJECTIVES

Diagnosis and Treatment Planning

At the end of this course, students will be proficient at many things related to diagnosis and treatment planning. They will be able to identify the principles of the diagnostic process as well as be able to use the *DSM-5* as a diagnostic tool. Students will be able to explain diagnostic criteria for mental, emotional, and personality disorders. They will also be able to describe treatment modalities within a client's range of care. Students will understand how culture and society influence diagnosis and the treatment planning process. They will also be able to describe competencies such as case conceptualization, diagnosis, treatment planning, and referrals. In addition, students will be able to develop personalized treatment plans for clients.

Assessment

At the end of this course, students will understand the role of assessment in the counseling process. They will be able to differentiate the appropriateness of assessment process and procedures for specific situations and populations. Students will leave the class with basic knowledge of statistical and measurement concepts, as well as be able to identify an assessment's reliability, validity, and its relationship to clients' race, gender, ethnicity, and age. In addition, students will understand how to interpret and disseminate results of assessments to clients and related individuals.

MUST-COVER TOPICS

This section identifies the important topics discussed in both the diagnosis and treatment planning course and the assessment course.

Diagnosis and Treatment Planning

In this course, counselor educators are connecting the dots for students regarding how symptoms influence diagnosis and how the diagnosis influences the treatment plan. To connect these dots, counselor educators need to consider covering some of these topics:

- The importance of diagnosis
- Diagnostic systems
- Diagnostic categories
- Making a diagnosis
- Diagnostic decision trees
- Diagnostic criteria for disorders such as:
  - Neurodevelopmental disorders
  - Schizophrenia spectrum and other psychotic disorders
  - Bipolar and related disorders
  - Depressive disorders
  - Anxiety disorders

- ○ Obsessive-compulsive and related disorders
- ○ Trauma- and stressor-related disorders
- ○ Dissociative disorders
- ○ Somatic symptom and related disorders
- ○ Feeding and eating disorders
- ○ Elimination disorders
- ○ Sleep–wake disorders
- ○ Sexual dysfunctions
- ○ Gender dysphoria
- ○ Disruptive, impulse-control, and conduct disorders
- ○ Substance-related and addictive disorders
- ○ Neurocognitive disorders
- ○ Personality disorders
- ○ Paraphilic disorders
- ○ Other mental disorders
- ○ Medication-induced movement disorders
- ○ Other conditions that may be focus of clinical attention
- Case conceptualization
- Treatment goals
- Objectives
- Interventions
- Long-term goals
- Short-term goals
- Theory-based interventions

Assessment

Assessments are powerful tools in the therapeutic process. This course helps students understand this tool and its benefits more in-depth. Covering the following topics can help counselor educators better prepare to teach this course:

- Purpose of Assessments in Counseling
- The Assessment Process

- Types of Assessments
- Evaluating Outcomes
- Professional, Legal, and Ethical Issues
- Multicultural Factors in Assessment
- Reliability
- Validity
- Scales of Measurement
- Raw Scores
- Mental Status Examination
- Intake Interview
- Suicide Assessment
- Substance Abuse Assessment
- Achievement Testing
- Intelligence Assessment
- Career Assessments
- Personality Assessments
- Relational Assessments
- Dissemination of Assessment Results

PERSONAL EXPERIENCE

The following sections include our personal experiences teaching these courses.

Teaching Approach

Both Diagnosis and Treatment Planning courses and Assessment courses are combination or connect-the-dot courses. This means that students will take skills from other courses and combine them with new information to inform their clinical work. As a result, we approach these classes as practical training courses as opposed to heavy lecture courses. Every class is filled with about 20% lecture and 80% practicing the skills. We also spend a significant part of lectures connecting the dots between assessments, diagnosis, and treatment planning. Helping students understand how these elements of the therapeutic process fit together enhances their learning process.

Student Experience

Diagnosis tends to be a value-laden topic for students. There is also a mixture of anxiety and fear regarding labeling a client with a diagnosis. It may be one of the first times students genuinely recognize their power as clinicians. It can be helpful to process their thoughts and feelings surrounding diagnosing. We try to focus on how, when done therapeutically, diagnosing clients can serve their treatment. In regard to treatment planning, we have found that this tends to be a weakness of students throughout their graduate school experience. Students struggle to identify goals, make the goals personalized for the clients, and use the appropriate interventions to help the clients reach their goals. This struggle can be attributed to a struggle to identify a theoretical orientation so sessions seem aimless. It can also stem from students not fully understanding the assessment process. The assessment process can be intimidating to students. They view the assessment course and research lightly. Any course that covers validity and reliability sends up red flags in students' minds. Easing their defensiveness by presenting the information from a practical perspective can help students understand how these elements work together.

Course Preparation

Much of the course preparation involves making the classes practical. This course should be more than covering each assessment procedure, diagnosis, and approach to treatment planning. Students need to be able to practice these elements of the counseling process. We prepare for these courses by printing assessments or parts of assessments for students' practice in class. We also prepare brief lectures providing additional information on diagnoses. We then prepare mock cases for students to practice identifying symptoms, potential approaches to treatment, and treatment planning. These cases can be found in any number of *DSM-5* casebooks. In sum, we prepare the assessments students will use to practice with in class, information regarding specific diagnoses, and then a mock case where they can practice diagnosing and developing short-term and long-term goals.

Nuts and Bolts

This preparation supports the in-class experience. If a class for either course takes place Thursday and today is Monday, the preparation for elements discussed in the previous session begins. For example, in the Diagnosis and Treatment Planning course, the mock case drives the lecture. If a class is 3 hours long, we spend 1 hour lecturing on the day's reading topic. Then the rest of the class is spent reading a case together as a class and discussing the client's symptoms until we can make a provisional and principal diagnosis. This is a time where students can ask specific "what if" questions. The assessment course classes are similar in that we spend some time focusing on content related to assessment processes and procedures. Then we practice selecting and administering assessments, both formal and informal.

Advice

When teaching the Diagnosis and Treatment Planning course, we suggest counselor educators be mindful of the following:

- Address the values surrounding diagnoses.
- Attend to the anxiety of the decision to diagnose a client.
- Focus on the connection between assessment, diagnosis, and treatment planning.

- Make the course practical, so much so that students fall into a rhythm of recognizing symptoms, identifying and conducting appropriate assessments, and using the results to co-construct treatment plans.
- Share personal experiences of diagnosing and treatment planning that succeeded and times when it was a struggle.

COURSE CONSIDERATIONS

Additional Textbooks

The following textbooks can be considered when preparing to teach the Diagnosis and Treatment Planning course:

- *Diagnostic and Statistical Manual of Mental Disorders, 5th Edition: DSM-5*, by American Psychiatric Association (2013)
- *Treating Those With Mental Disorders: A Comprehensive Approach to Case Conceptualization and Treatment*, by Victoria E. Kress and Matthew J. Paylo (2018)
- *The Complete Adult Psychotherapy Treatment Planner*, by Arthur E. Jongsma Jr., L. Mark Peterson, and Timothy J. Bruce (2014)
- *Theory and Treatment Planning in Counseling and Psychotherapy*, by Diane R. Gehart (2015)
- *Theory-Based Treatment Planning for Marriage and Family Therapists: Integrating Theory and Practice*, by Diane R. Gehart and Amy R. Tuttle (2002)

The following textbooks can be considered when preparing to teach the Assessment course:

- *Assessment Procedures for Counselors and Helping Professionals* (8th Edition; Merrill Counselling),

by Robert J. Drummond, Carl J. Sheperis, and Karyn D. Jones (2015)
- *Assessment in Counseling: Procedures and Practices*, by Danica G. Hays (2017)
- *Assessment Procedures for Counselors and Helping Professionals*, by Carl J. Sheperis, Robert J. Drummond, and Karyn D. Jones (2019)
- *Essentials of Testing and Assessment: A Practical Guide for Counselors, Social Workers, and Psychologists*, by Edward S. Neukrug and R. Charles Fawcett (2014)

Mock Schedule

A potential course schedule and class topics may look like the examples in Exhibits 11.1 and 11.2.

EXHIBIT 11.1 Diagnosis, Assessment, and Treatment Planning Course: Mock Schedule

Date	Course Content
Aug 27	Introduction to the Course: Assessment & Diagnosis
Sep 3	Etiology and Documentation & Treatment Planning Other conditions that may be a focus of clinical attention (*DSM-5*, p. 715*)
Sep 10	Neurodevelopmental Disorders (*DSM-5*, p. 31)
Sep 17	Bipolar and Related Disorders/Depressive Disorders (*DSM-5*, pp. 123 and 155)
Sep 24	Schizophrenia Spectrum and Other Psychotic Disorders (*DSM-5*, p. 87)
Oct 1	Sleep–Wake Disorders (*DSM-5*, p. 361)

(*continued*)

EXHIBIT 11.1 Diagnosis, Assessment, and Treatment Planning Course: Mock Schedule (*continued*)

Date	Course Content
Oct 8	Anxiety disorders (*DSM-5*, p. 189) Somatic Symptom and Related Disorders (*DSM-5*, p. 309)
Oct 15	Obsessive-Compulsive and Related Disorders (*DSM-5*, p. 235)
Oct 22	Dissociative Disorders (*DSM-5*, p. 291)
Oct 29	Sexual Disorders and Gender Dysphoria (*DSM-5*, pp. 423 and 451)
Nov 5	Feeding and Eating disorders (*DSM-5*, p. 329) Elimination Disorders (*DSM-5*, p. 355)
Nov 12	Personality Disorders (*DSM-5*, p. 645)
Nov 19	Trauma- and Stressor-Related Disorders (*DSM-5*, p. 265)
Nov 26	Neurocognitive Disorders (Delirium, Dementia, Amnestic, and Other Cognitive Disorders) (*DSM-5*, p. 591)
Dec 3	Other Mental Disorders/Medication Movement Disorders (*DSM-5*, pp. 707 and 709)
Dec 10	Final Exam

*Listed readings refer to American Psychiatric Association. (2013). *Diagnostic and statistical manual of mental disorders* (5th ed.). Arlington, VA: American Psychiatric Publishing.

EXHIBIT 11.2 Diagnosis, Assessment, and Treatment Planning Course: Class Topics

Class #	Topic
1	Review of Syllabus History of Testing and Assessment
2	Diagnosis in the Assessment Process The Assessment Report Process

(*continued*)

EXHIBIT 11.2 Diagnosis, Assessment, and Treatment Planning Course: Class Topics (*continued*)

Class #	Topic
3	Validity, Reliability, Practicality, and Cross-Cultural Fairness
4	Making Meaning out of Test Scores
5	Deriving Meaning out of Test Scores
6	Making Meaning out of Test Scores
7	Making Meaning out of Test Scores
8	Midterm Exam
9	Career and Occupational Assessment: Interest Inventories, Special and Multiple Aptitude Testing
10	Educational Assessment of Ability: Readiness, Survey Battery, Diagnostic
11	Intellectual and Cognitive Functioning: Intelligence Testing and Neuropsychological Assessment
12	Objective and Projective Testing
13	Informal Assessment
14	Test Report Reviews
15	Final Exam

Note: Schedule is based on Neukrug, E. S., & Fawcett, R. C. (2014). *Essentials of testing and assessment: A practical guide for counselors, social workers, and psychologists*. Boston, MA: Cengage Learning.

COURSE ASSIGNMENTS

Diagnosis and Treatment Planning

Diagnostic vignette. Students will choose a diagnostic condition around which a case vignette will be constructed. This should be a two- to four-paragraph vignette that provides enough information to comprehensively identify how a client may be impaired by his or her diagnosis. Once students have chosen their diagnosis, they will be asked to do the following:

- Complete a comprehensive narrative providing support for the diagnosis as well as all ways in which the client is impaired by his or her condition.
- Construct an informal treatment plan including goals and methods to accomplish those goals.
- Provide a record of any additional documentation and/or referrals (if you deem appropriate for the client).

Assessment

Assessment battery report. Students are to complete a four- to six-page report that summarizes the results of a series of assessments completed during a clinical interview with an individual. Students must use a minimum of three tests or assessment instruments. The report should include all assessment categories listed in Box 4.5, pp. 75–76, of Chapter 4 of the text (see Table 11.1 for examples). This assignment is created using the text *Essentials of Testing and Assessment: A Practical Guide for Counselors, Social Workers, and Psychologists*, by Edward S. Neukrug and R. Charles Fawcett (2014).

TABLE 11.1 Assessments for Late Adolescents/Adults and Children

Tests for Late Adolescents or Adults	Tests for Children
Beck Depression Inventory (or BAI)	Child's Grades
Beck Anxiety Inventory (or BDI)	WRAT-III

(continued)

TABLE 11.1 Assessments for Late Adolescents/Adults and Children (*continued*)

Tests for Late Adolescents or Adults	Tests for Children
SASSI	Coopersmith
16PF	KFD
WRAT-III	Sentence Completion
KFD or Sentence Completion	Child's Recent Achievement Test Scores
Myers–Briggs	O*NET Profiler: Short or Long Form
O*NET Profiler: Short or Long Form	Self-Directed Search (SDS)
Career Rating Scale	

Source: Neukrug, E. S., & Fawcett, R. C. (2014). *Essentials of testing and assessment: A practical guide for counselors, social workers, and psychologists*. Boston, MA: Cengage Learning.

Note: 16PF, The Sixteen Personality Factor Questionnaire; KFD, kinetic family drawings; O*NET, occupational information network; SASSI, Substance Abuse Subtle Screening Inventory; WRAT-III, Wide Range Achievement Test.

REFERENCES

American Psychiatric Association. (2013). *Diagnostic and statistical manual of mental disorders* (5th ed.). Arlington, VA: American Psychiatric Publishing.

Neukrug, E. S., & Fawcett, R. C. (2014). *Essentials of testing and assessment: A practical guide for counselors, social workers, and psychologists*. Boston, MA: Cengage Learning.

INTRODUCTION

Clinical courses such as Practicum and Internship can be the cornerstone of a program. Students' value to the communities they serve is heavily influenced by the training students receive throughout their practicum and internship training. Students pass through many gates to make it to the clinical portion of the program. They have been monitored and evaluated by most faculty and deemed ready to work with live clients. It is the job of the practicum and internship instructors to push a student to grow into the potential that has been cultivated throughout the program. Teaching these courses often involves more work than other courses in the curriculum.

COURSE DESCRIPTION

This is the course that a majority of the new counselor educators look forward to teaching but may never get a chance because tenured faculty members have worked themselves into the rotation. If given the chance, new counselor educators need to beware because this course packs a punch. Council for Accreditation of Counseling and Related Educational Programs (CACREP) should rename these courses "Paperwork" instead of Practicum and Internship. Essentially, during the practicum and internship experience, students work with clients at a clinical site or placement for a semester. While it is in the counselor educator's responsibility to fill up a student's schedule with clients, it is his or her job to help students make the training experience meaningful. These courses are taught in a variety of ways in counselor education programs. Some students are sent away from the program to complete their practicum experience at an external site. These students may be supervised by doctoral students and/or external site supervisors. Some programs have an onsite clinic where students can work with clients without having to use external sites. Almost every internship student seeks an external site to complete his or her internship experience.

During practicum and internship, students meet weekly with faculty for individual supervision and group supervision over the semester. Students are also expected to spend additional time outside of supervision meetings each week completing paperwork and managing their caseload. In Practicum, students are required to accrue a minimum of 100 direct and indirect hours related to their on- and off-campus placement sites. Practicum is the first of three clinical instruction courses offering supervised clinical practice in counseling skills, behaviors, professional orientation/dispositions, and assessment. Primary emphasis is on performing counseling and related activities in a specified agency, school, church, or community clinical mental health setting.

The Internship course is separated into two courses taken after practicum and in two semesters. Most programs call these courses Internship I and II. During each Internship semester, interns will complete 300 clock hours of supervised internship experiences, 120 of which are direct service and 180 indirect service. They will receive a minimum of 1 hour per week of individual or triadic supervision by their external site supervisor and a minimum of 1 hour per week of individual or triadic supervision by the faculty or doctoral supervisor, and they will attend 1.5 hours per week of group supervision provided by the faculty supervisor.

COURSE OBJECTIVES

When this course is completed, students will be able to demonstrate professionalism in both orientation and disposition. They will also have a defined professional identity as a clinical mental health counselor, school counselor, or marriage and family therapist. Students will also be evaluated using the Counseling Competencies Scale (CCS). Students will demonstrate professional competency at a minimum of 6.0 in Primary Counseling Skills, Professional Disposition, and Professional Behaviors as defined in the CCS. Students will also be able to recognize their level of competence and limitations in the counseling process. Students will be able to show their understanding of and the ability to apply ethical and legal concerns in clinical mental health counseling or marriage, couple, and family counseling, and school counseling. Students will engage professionally and ethically in a variety of professional activities, including direct counseling service, record keeping, supervision, information and referral, in-service training, and staff meetings. Students will demonstrate their knowledge of assessment instruments, treatment planning, diagnosis, and interventions. Students will demonstrate their skills in conducting intake interview, mental status evaluation, biopsychosocial history, mental health history, systems assessment models, and psychological assessment. Students will put all the educational pieces of their curriculum to use in practicum and internship.

MUST-COVER TOPICS

The Practicum and Internship courses are not like traditional lecture-style courses. An essential purpose of class meetings is to conduct group supervision. Supervision does not often leave time to review PowerPoint slides. However, counselor educators find ways to cover some important topics such as:

- The CCS, which assesses students' skill development and professional competencies. The CCS also helps counselor educators provide direct feedback to their students.
- Clinical Assessment and Progress Note
- Suicide/Homicide Issues
- Client Behaviors
- Case Conceptualization
- Counselor's Development
- Treatment Planning
- Case Transfer and Termination
- Mental Status Exams
- Client Assessment
- Required Documentation
- Client Boundaries
- Domestic Violence
- Referrals & Collaboration With Other Professionals

As stated earlier, these topics are difficult to cover in addition to the clinical issues covered in class. Some counselor educators allot 30 minutes during class time to discuss these topics. Other counselor educators use the course's online platform to create learning modules for students regarding these topics.

PERSONAL EXPERIENCE

Teaching Approach

We wear many different hats when teaching the Practicum and Internship courses. As instructors, we share with students information on the must-cover topics listed earlier. As supervisors we work with students to provide the highest level of care they can provide their clients. We do not counsel our students, but we use counseling skills to process personal issues related to students' caseloads. As professionals we act as gatekeepers for the profession, protecting the public from counselors who may cause them harm or cause themselves harm. We approach this course trying to integrate all of these roles. We are open with students about them and what it means for our relationship. We do not lecture in this course. We both chose to create online modules for students that cover the important topics listed previously. Also included in the online platform of these courses are discussion questions, important files, and videos that enhance student learning. When students come to class, we are free to process cases that challenge them. We try to integrate the topic of the day into the clinical processing but work not to force the topic. We have found that students, especially practicum students, use the class as home base. They face their fears and anxieties seeing clients throughout the week knowing that they will have the class to check in and breathe.

Course Preparation

The preparation for this course is front loaded. Before the semester starts, we grab our supervisees' clinical files. If we are teaching Internship, we look through the previous semester's CCS to familiarize ourselves with students' strengths and growth areas. We develop the course's online platform, inputting videos, discussion questions, and documents. We then ensure that we have all of the current documentation our program needs placed in each student's clinical file at the end of the semester. We also prepare the classroom for confidentiality, buying sound machines and covering door windows. If there is technology to use when viewing therapy sessions and clinical notes, we orient ourselves to them before the first supervision session or class meeting. As we discuss later, each class within these courses is set up the same. Students find their rhythm, sharing cases and processing their experiences.

Nuts and Bolts

As discussed, the nuts and bolts of these courses are fairly straightforward. Each week we prepare to meet with students individually for supervision and then as a group for supervision. During individual supervision, we keep track of paperwork, which is different for each program. We review treatment notes and plans. Then we start processing cases with students, discussing the technical and personal aspects of the therapeutic process. Practicum students may need more orientation and guidance regarding the clinical process. Some of the early supervision and class meetings may be focused more on these tasks. By Internship, students generally understand how to use supervision. They may have a better handle on the paperwork and managing a caseload.

We felt most helpful to students when we were able to stay organized. Students may submit hour's logs for us to sign and place into their clinical folders. Students may also have evaluations from their external site supervisors. We will have our own internal evaluations such as the CCS. All of this paperwork and signatures need to be organized and stored efficiently. These day-to-day assignments can build up, and papers can get misplaced, causing students to delay graduation because they are 1 hour short, or students may struggle to get licensed if paperwork is not up to date.

Advice

The following section outlines our advice when teaching the Practicum and Internship courses:

- Be mindful that students are overwhelmed. Packing the course with busy work will be

frustrating. We believe this course is best taught simply. This gives students the space to grow.
- Balance processing clinical issues and how those issues are personally influencing students' growth.
- Evaluate honestly so that the next supervisor knows where to start.
- Keep files up to date, with documents signed and organized.
- If external site visits are necessary, schedule those site visits early because external site supervisors are just as busy as you.
- Be a good supervisor. We make such a profound impact on students' clinical experience. Own that responsibility.

COURSE CONSIDERATIONS

Additional Textbooks

- *Practicum and Internship: Textbook and Resource Guide for Counseling and Psychotherapy*, by Christin M. Jungers (2019)
- *The Counseling Practicum and Internship Manual, Second Edition: A Resource for Graduate Counseling Students*, by Shannon Hodges (2015)
- *Internship, Practicum, and Field Placement Handbook*, by Brian Baird (2013)
- *Interpersonal Process in Therapy: An Integrative Model*, by Edward Teyber and Faith Teyber (2016)
- *Letters to a Young Therapist*, by Mary Pipher (2016)
- *The Gift of Therapy: An Open Letter to a New Generation of Therapists and Their Patients*, by Irvin Yalom (2017)
- *On Being a Therapist*, by Jeffrey Kottler (2017)

Mock Schedule

Practicum
A mock schedule for a practicum is illustrated in Exhibit 12.1.

EXHIBIT 12.1 Practicum Mock Schedule

Date	Topic	Reading* and Assignment Due
Jan 17	Overview of Course, Orientation & Contract	
Jan 24	Clinical Assessment and Progress Note	The Gift of Therapy 1–6 Weekly discussion post on "Clinical Assessment and Progress Note"
Jan 31	Suicide/Homicide Issues	The Gift of Therapy 7–13 Weekly discussion post on "Suicide/Homicide Issues"
Feb 7	Child Abuse and Reporting Issue	The Gift of Therapy 14–20 Weekly discussion post on "Child Abuse and Reporting Issue"
Feb 14	Practicum Counselor's Development	The Gift of Therapy 21–27 Weekly discussion post on "Practicum Counselor's Development"
Feb 21	Supervision Process group	The Gift of Therapy 28–34 Weekly discussion post on *a selected reading related to your cases*
Feb 28	Supervision Process group	The Gift of Therapy 35–41 Weekly discussion post on *a selected reading related to your cases*

(continued)

EXHIBIT 12.1 Practicum Mock Schedule (*continued*)

Date	Topic	Reading* and Assignment Due
Mar 7	Midterm CCS Review	The Gift of Therapy 42–48 Weekly discussion post on *a selected reading related to your cases*
Mar 14	Spring Break	
Mar 21	Supervision Process group	The Gift of Therapy 49–55 Weekly discussion post on *a selected reading related to your cases*
Mar 28	Supervision Process group	The Gift of Therapy 56–62 Weekly discussion post on *a selected reading related to your cases*
Apr 4	Case Transfer and Termination	The Gift of Therapy 63–69 Weekly discussion post on "Case Transfer and Termination"
Apr 11	Supervision Process group	The Gift of Therapy 70–76 Weekly discussion post on *a selected reading related to your cases*
Apr 18	Supervision Process group	The Gift of Therapy 77–83 Weekly discussion post on *a selected reading related to your cases*
Apr 25	Supervision Process group	The Gift of Therapy 84–85 Weekly discussion post on *a selected reading related to your cases*
May 2	Final CCS Review	Course Debriefing

*Listed readings refer to Yalom, I. (2017). *The gift of therapy: An open letter to a new generation of therapists and their patients.* New York, NY: Harper Perennial.

Internship

Exhibit 12.2 presents an example schedule for an internship.

EXHIBIT 12.2 Internship Mock Schedule

Week Of	Group Supervision	Individual Supervision
Aug 26	Introduction & Overview; confirm individual supervision day and time; review internship documents, CCS and Counselor Development; discuss Case Presentation schedule	*For all individual supervision:* Come to individual supervision prepared with a counseling session to review and discuss.
Sep 2	Labor Day	No Class
Sep 9	Topic: Professional Client Behaviors Case Presentation	Discuss Counselor Development Goals Form; all supervision forms completed Site Supervisor Brief Evaluation Due
Sep 16	Topic: Case Conceptualization Case Presentation	
Sep 23	Topic: Treatment Planning Case Presentation	Site Supervisor Brief Evaluation Due
Sep 30	Topic: Mental Status Exams (MSE) Case Presentation	
Oct 7	Topic: Client Assessment Case Presentation	Site Supervisor Brief Evaluation Due

(continued)

EXHIBIT 12.2 Internship Mock Schedule (*continued*)

Week Of	Group Supervision	Individual Supervision
Oct 14	Topic: Required Documentation Case Presentation	
Oct 21	Topic: Client Boundaries Case Presentation	CCS Midterm Faculty Evaluation Site Supervisor Brief Evaluation Due
Oct 28	Topic: Domestic Violence Case Presentation	
Nov 4	Topic: Suicide Assessment & Intervention Case Presentation	Site Supervisor Brief Evaluation Due
Nov 11	Topic: Transfers/ Term & Client Care Case Presentation	
Nov 18	Topic: Referrals & Collaboration With Other Professionals Case Presentation	Site Supervisor Brief Evaluation Due
Nov 25	Topic: Discussion About Clinical Portfolio Case Presentation	
Dec 2	In-Class Presentations of Professional Portfolios	CCS Final Faculty Evaluation Site Supervisor Brief Evaluation Due
Dec 9	Class does not meet; individual supervision still occurs	*Final Chart Audits*

CCS, Counseling Competencies Scale.

COURSE ASSIGNMENTS

Practicum

Video session review. Students will review two of their own recorded counseling sessions from the first half of the semester and complete a Clinical Self-Rating Form and reflection paper for each reviewed session. Students will then review two of their own recorded counseling sessions from the second half of the semester and complete a Clinical Self-Rating Form for each reviewed session.

    Master's counseling sessions. Students will review two Master's Counseling Sessions (available on DVD at the library) and write a reflection paper for each reviewed session. Students will provide a personal account of how the master's theory either matches or conflicts with their clinical experience. This will be both philosophical and practical in nature. Students can reference clinical experiences without identifying information about clients. Each reflection paper will be no less than two content pages in length, providing appropriate references when needed.

    Weekly article review. Students will review one professional journal article that addresses clinical issues encountered during the Practicum class. Students will provide a half-page reflection on the article and post the reflection along with the professional article in the "Weekly Article Discussion" on the learning management system (LMS). Students will also post comments for two other students' reviews weekly. These articles will be measured via the CCS.

Internship

Clinical portfolio. Students may choose to submit this portfolio online or inside a binder. The following are the portfolio components:

1. Professional identity
   a. Résumé (vita) and personal statement (cover letter)
   b. Licensed Professional Counselor (LPC)/ Marriage and Family Therapy (MFT) licensure information with completed practicum experience verification form
   c. Texas LPC/MFT rules and regulations
   d. Malpractice insurance information addressing clients' rights
   e. Supervision information: current (and past) supervisors and qualifications
2. Professional development
   a. Membership in professional organizations, for example, MTCA, TCA, TAMFT, CCT, ACA, or AAMFT
   b. Conferences(s)/workshops/trainings attended
   c. Presentations
   d. Continuing education
3. Professional practice
   a. Web link and resources for counselors/clients
   b. Psychopharmacological information links
4. Other
   a. Volunteer/mentorship activities
   b. Letters of recommendation

13 MARRIAGE, COUPLE, AND FAMILY COUNSELING COURSES

INTRODUCTION

Some counselor education programs have a Clinical Mental Health Counseling (CMHC) track and either a School Counseling or Marriage, Family, and Child Counseling (MFCC) track. Other programs may have all three and a nonclinical track from which students may choose. This chapter focuses on courses taught in the MFCC track. It is not within the scope of this book to focus on each course taught in this track. Our hope is to summarize some of the most helpful information to consider when prepping to teach a course in this track.

COURSE DESCRIPTION

Courses in the MFCC track can be intimidating for some students. While these courses teach students how to recognize and intervene in the unhealthy systemic patterns within their clients' lives, they also invite students to do the same in their own lives. Each class in every course might leave students reflecting on their own relationships with their family of origin (FOO), partner, and children. These classes can be the first ones where students recognize multigenerational issues and their effects on their relationships today, in addition to the personal reflective experience throughout the courses in this track. Working with multiple individuals in the room and managing the relational processing are concerns for students. Being comfortable in this setting takes training; it is a gradual process. It takes time to learn how to juggle multiple therapeutic processes effectively. Typically, MFCC students take the same basic courses as CMHC students. These courses are covered in previous chapters. Then the students separate into smaller cohorts and take track-specific courses. The timing of this separation is program specific. Some of the track-specific courses might include Brief Counseling Interventions, Couple's Counseling, Counseling Children and Adolescents, Marriage and Family Therapy Assessment, and Advanced Marriage and Family Techniques. In most cases, track-specific courses might make up about 12 hours of students' 60 credit hour curriculum.

COURSE OBJECTIVES

Courses in this track attempt to provide students with the attitude, knowledge, and skill to work with family, couples, and children. Each course will focus on a specific aspect of working with this population. A course in Brief Counseling Interventions will focus on solution-focused techniques with families. Students will be trained to work with families on a short-term basis. This includes quick but in-depth assessments, goal setting, and interventions that help couples and families achieve their treatment goals. A course in Couple's Counseling will examine common areas and patterns of marital dysfunction. This course may focus on specific techniques and interventions for working with couples at different stages of their relationship. Students might walk away from a couple's course with the ability to distinguish the couple as its own subsystem within a family. They will be able to describe how problems occur within a couple's relationship and how change occurs. Students will be able to demonstrate couple counseling skills as well as be able to identify how each partner brings influences from his or her family, culture, and society into the relationship. Counseling Children and Adolescents courses apply the relevant theories and techniques to child and adolescent populations. Students become familiar with the emotional and behavioral disorders common among this population and focus on using evidence-based practices with this population. They also understand the cultural, developmental, and environmental factors that impact childhood and adolescent treatment. Marriage and Family Therapy Assessment courses introduce students to assessing the system. This course also focuses on the technical aspects of the MFCC sessions, such as diagnostic interviews, genograms, family mapping, mental diagnostic status examinations, symptom inventories, and psychoeducational and personality assessment. Advanced Marriage and Family Techniques courses deepen students' knowledge of theories and how to apply them in practice. This course is designed to build upon students' knowledge from courses such as Marriage and Family Therapy Theories, Marriage and Family Therapy Assessment, Couple's Counseling, and Counseling Children and Adolescents.

MUST-COVER TOPICS

Within all of these courses, there are must-cover topics that students in the Marriage and Family Therapy (MFT) track need to know to graduate. Here, we identify some of these topics and briefly describe a few as well. Some of the must-cover topics in these courses are the following:

- Ethics in Marriage and Family Therapy
  (In addition to the American Counseling Association's Code of Ethics, MFCC students need to familiarize themselves with state laws and the American Association for Marriage and Family Therapy code of ethics.)

- Research and Evidence-Based Practices
- Marriage and Family Therapy Theories
  - Systemic and Strategic Therapies
  - Structural Family Therapy
  - Experiential Approaches
  - Intergenerational Family Therapy Approaches
  - Cognitive-Behavioral Approaches
  - Solution-Based Approaches
  - Narrative and Collaborative Approaches
- Ways of conducting an MFCC therapy session (The therapeutic process looks different when sitting with a couple, family, or child, so students need to know the practical ways of conducting an MFCC therapy session.)
  - Case conceptualizations
  - Conducting clinical assessments
  - Treatment planning
  - Evaluation of progress
  - Completing documentation
- Other topics
  - Family structure (This is important to discuss with students because this topic is often value laden. Students need to process the meaning of family and understand healthy family structures.)
  - Boundaries
  - Hierarchy
  - Symmetrical and complementary relationships
  - Interactional patterns
  - Intergenerational
  - Attachment styles
  - Feedback loops
  - Genogram (Students need to learn how to construct and read genograms conversationally. Constructing a genogram with clients can also be a great way to solidify the therapeutic relationship. Sometimes

students focus too much on completing the task that they lose sight of the process.)
o Dominant discourses

PERSONAL EXPERIENCE

We have the luxury of teaching courses in both the CMHC and MFCC tracks at our universities. Between us, we have prepped for many standard courses offered in the MFCC track. The following sections include our experience prepping for and teaching these courses.

Teaching Approach

We have found that students carry a significant amount of anxiety into each course in this track. Most of their anxiety revolves around making mistakes that might cause some unforeseen harm to the family, such as splitting them apart, missing something important, or causing emotional harm to the children in counseling. Our approach in these courses is to build students' confidence as well as their knowledge, skills, and activities. Each course in this track is taught differently. Marriage and Family Therapy Theories courses are typically taught traditionally, using PowerPoint lectures and rarely using experiential activities. As the courses become more practical, the teaching approaches parallel this shift. For example, Advanced Marriage and Family Techniques courses are taught using almost no lecture components, and instead, students practice and receive feedback. Regardless of the course, students' anxieties about working with families need to be addressed.

In addition to addressing students' anxieties, the process of working with families needs to be broken down in ways that students are able to integrate into how they are in session. Each course focuses on a specific aspect of the therapeutic process of marriage, family, and child counseling. Sometimes it takes drawing genograms on the board for 2 hours as students make up family systems to understand genograms. It may also be helpful to draw positive and negative feedback loops on the board using most family interactions. Students can benefit from seeing these complex MFCC ideas and interacting with them.

Another aspect of our approach when teaching these courses is making it personal. Joining with a family is a personal endeavor. In order to do this, students do much of their personal growing through the assignments in these courses. We dive into the theories and techniques that help families grow closer together. While doing so, most students reflect upon their own families and relationships. We do not shy away from this in class, often inviting students to filter lectures and conversations through their own families and relationships. When discussing differentiation, we ask them to think about their own FOOs and the level of differentiation within their system.

We teach these courses with a mixture of PowerPoint lectures, open class discussion, and experiential activities. Theories courses are usually heavy lecture classes because of the amount of information students need to consume to be prepared for their next courses. A course such as Advanced MFT Techniques is better taught using experiential activities so students can see and feel how these techniques are conducted. However, we have found the MFT Assessment is better taught without PowerPoint lectures but through class discussions led by the course's text. This gives students a better opportunity to ask questions and debate some of the important points of MFCC.

Student Experience

As we discussed, students experience these courses with mixed feelings of excitement and anxiety. Some classes have similar life experiences and use these experiences in class as examples. They help each other understand concepts, and some students gain small "aha" moments in classes. We have stressed breaking down the concepts discussed in these courses because they are complex. In our experience, MFCC students struggle to integrate some of the ideas. This is especially true when students have not seen clients yet. Students tend to have more exposure to CMHC ideas and approaches from undergrad courses and possibly books that have interested them up until graduate school. Training students how to recognize positive and negative feedback loops in a couple's argument can be more difficult for some because it is the first time they are being introduced to the concept. Sometimes, this frustration can cause students to leave the MFCC track to another.

Students can also have high emotional reactivity toward some of the discussions in class. As we mentioned, sometimes students experience "aha" moments in classes that make them question the health of their relationships. Some students may recognize how they are contributing to unhealthy relationships. Other students might suddenly realize why a marriage ended in divorce or why their parents' marriage ended the same way as theirs. Honestly, students' experience of these courses are unpredictable. The content hits home for many students who chose to come to the program to help clients going through some of the things students themselves went through within their families of origin. Counselor educators have to be mindful of the deep personal aspects of these courses when teaching.

Course Preparation

Courses in the MFCC track take a considerable amount of time to prepare. Like marriage, family, and child counseling, these courses are a spider web of processes. All lectures need to be purged of overly complicated ideas and explanations to make room for down-to-earth discussions. Some of our courses are taught from 6:00 p.m. to 8:50 p.m., after students have worked all day long. If they come to class and have us try to explain cybernetics and cybernetics of cybernetics through a dry, boring lecture, they will not understand it. Counselor educators need to meet students where they are when preparing to explain these concepts.

Some of the challenges we face when prepping for this course are breaking down the complexity of topics and managing students' personal issues in class. Most of our efforts when prepping for this course go into finding clear ways of explaining concepts to students. We look for videos, use case examples and personal stories, and ask students to use their real-life examples. Oftentimes, this last way fuels students struggling with their personal issues in class. In our first couple of times teaching MFCC courses, we asked for volunteers without completely considering what might be shared in a genogram, sculpting, or feedback loop activity. This caused some students to overshare or become triggered when unprepared for how revealing these activities can become. We now put constraints around activities to help students share safely. We are also more prepared to discuss with students what things are safe to share and what might be too much. As with other classes outside of the MFCC track, these courses need to be prepared for with intentionality.

Nuts and Bolts

Staying on track in these courses can prove challenging sometimes. As discussed, students often see themselves and their families in the theories, topics, and activities. Talking to students about staying on track before classes where we knew the content could encourage emotion-filled discussions helps to stay focused. We also plan for extra processing time after an activity or demonstration in class. Processing can take longer because of the complexity of the therapeutic process. Also, doing activities with families or couples may lead to more technical and "what if" questions from students. The assignments in these courses, especially the creative assignments such as creating a genogram or family eco-map, need detailed instructions and rubrics. The best thing about these assignments is that students can be creative. It is sometimes difficult to grade assignments when they are so varied in presentation. Providing instruction and rubrics can help students express themselves while allowing the grading to remain objective.

Advice

In this section, like previous chapters, we share our advice when teaching courses in the MFCC track:

- Do your own systems work in therapy. Explore your FOO and how those interactions influence your relationships. Figure out your trigger points so you can avoid them in the class when students ask questions.
- Practice constructing genograms and feedback loops until you can do them in your sleep.
- Hold a small caseload of couples and families. We have found that seeing couples and families while teaching these courses has kept us sharp.
- Complete the assignments yourself to make sure all of the kinks are worked out. Some assignments are multistep projects that can be confusing.
- Provide students with lecture notes they can use to study for the licensure exam.
- Make the class practical and the content covered down to earth.

- Provide boundaries for student sharing in class to keep students safe.
- Explain the differences between a Licensed Marriage and Family Therapist (LMFT) and Licensed Professional Counselor (LPC).
- Attend to students' anxieties around working with couples, families, and children.
- Be aware of the multiple processes going on within the classroom: students who are more affected by topics, those who need more support, and those who struggle to see things systemically.

COURSE CONSIDERATIONS

Additional Textbooks

The following list includes suggested textbooks used for courses in the MFCC track:

- *Mastering Competencies in Family Therapy: A Practical Approach to Theory and Clinical Case Documentation*, by Diane R. Gehart (2017)
- *Family Therapy: History, Theory, and Practice*, by Samuel T. Gladding (2018)
- *Theory-Based Treatment Planning for Marriage and Family Therapists: Integrating Theory and Practice*, by Diane R. Gehart and Amy R. Tuttle (2002)
- *Doing Family Therapy, Third Edition: Craft and Creativity in Clinical Practice*, by Robert Taibbi (2015)
- *Couple and Family Assessment*, by Len Sperry (2019)
- *Family Assessment Handbook: An Introduction and Practical Guide to Family Assessment*, by Barbara Thomlison (2015)

- *Diversity in Couple and Family Therapy: Ethnicities, Sexualities, and Socioeconomics*, by Shalonda Kelly (2016)
- *Case Conceptualization in Family Therapy*, by Michael D. Reiter (2013)
- *Common Factors in Couple and Family Therapy: The Overlooked Foundation for Effective Practice*, by Douglas H. Sprenkle, Sean D. Davis, and Jay L. Lebow (2013)
- *Family Therapy: A Systemic Integration*, by D. S. Becvar and R. J. Becvar (2013)

Mock Schedule

The following are a couple of different examples of potential schedules from various courses in the MFCC track.

The mock schedule for Marriage and Family Therapy Assessment presented in Exhibit 13.1 was developed as if *Family Assessment Handbook: An Introductory Practice Guide to Family Assessment*, by Barbara Thomlison, and *Mastering Competencies in Family Therapy: A Practical Approach to Theory and Clinical Case Documentation*, by Diane R. Gehart, were the course textbooks.

EXHIBIT 13.1 Marriage and Family Therapy Assessment: Mock Schedule A

Date	Topics	Readings* and Assignments
Aug 23	Introduction to Course Discussion of Assignments and Grading	Syllabus
Aug 30	Family Contexts: Getting Started in Family Assessment	Chapter 1, Thomlison

(*continued*)

EXHIBIT 13.1 Marriage and Family Therapy
Assessment: Mock Schedule A (*continued*)

Date	Topics	Readings* and Assignments
Sep 6	A Framework for Understanding Families	Chapter 2, Thomlison
Sep 13	The Family System	Chapter 3, Thomlison
Sep 20	Core Task of Family Assessment	Chapter 4, Thomlison
Sep 27	Clinical Assessment	Chapter 14, Gehart
Oct 4	Selecting Family Assessment Instruments to Evaluate Change	Chapter 9, Thomlison
Oct 11	Case Conceptualization	Chapter 13, Gehart
Oct 18	Older Adults, Families, and Life Stressors Family-Centered Interventions for Coping With Difficult Life Stressors Cognitive and Behavioral Strategies for Supporting and Strengthening Families	Chapters 6–8, Thomlison
Oct 25	Setting Goals and Selecting Family Interventions	Chapter 5, Thomlison
Nov 1	Treatment Planning	Chapter 15, Gehart
Nov 8	Evaluating Progress in Therapy	Chapter 16, Gehart
Nov 15	Document It: Progress Notes	Chapter 17, Gehart
Nov 22	Thanksgiving	No Class

(*continued*)

EXHIBIT 13.1 Marriage and Family Therapy Assessment: Mock Schedule A (*continued*)

Date	Topics	Readings* and Assignments
Nov 29	The Role of Reflection and Disclosure Writing Skills for Engaging With Families	Chapters 10 and 11, Thomlison
Dec 6	Final Exam	

*Listed readings refer to Thomlison, B. (2015). *Family assessment handbook: An introduction and practical guide to family assessment*. Boston, MA: Cengage Learning; Gehart, D. R. (2017). *Mastering competencies in family therapy: A practical approach to theory and clinical case documentation*. Boston, MA: Cengage Learning.

The mock schedule for Marriage and Family Therapy Theories shown in Exhibit 13.2 was developed as if *Family Therapy: A Systemic Integration*, by D. S. Becvar and R. J. Becvar, and *Mastering Competencies in Family Therapy: A Practical Approach to Theory and Clinical Case Documentation*, by Diane R. Gehart, were the course textbooks.

EXHIBIT 13.2 Marriage and Family Therapy Theories: Mock Schedule B

Date	Topic	Reading*
Jan 15	Introduce MFT Worldviews and History	Chapters 1 and 2, Becvar Chapters 1 and 2, Gehart
Jan 22	System Thinking and Postmodernism	Chapters 3 and 4, Becvar Chapter 3, Gehart
Jan 29	Family Process and Conceptualization	Chapter 5, Becvar Chapter 13, Gehart

(*continued*)

EXHIBIT 13.2 Marriage and Family Therapy Theories: Mock Schedule B (*continued*)

Date	Topic	Reading*
Feb 5	Psychodynamic (Relational Ethic/ Object Relations)	Chapter 6, Becvar Chapter 7 (pp. 243–274), Gehart
Feb 12	Natural System (Bowen)	Chapter 7, Becvar Chapter 7 (pp. 229–242), Gehart
Feb 19	After-Exam Review	
Feb 26	Communication (MRI)	Chapter 10 (pp. 193–199), Becvar Chapter 4 (pp. 61–87), Gehart
Mar 5	Experiential (Satir)	Chapter 10 (pp. 200–206), Becvar Chapter 6 (pp. 166–179), Gehart
Mar 12	Spring Break	
Mar 19	Structural	Chapter 9, Becvar Chapter 5, Gehart
Mar 26	Strategic and Milan	Chapter 11, Becvar Chapter 4 (pp. 75–124), Gehart
Apr 2	After-Exam Review	
Apr 9	Behavioral/ Cognitive	Chapter 12, Becvar Chapter 8, Gehart
Apr 16	Postmodern (Solution Based)	Chapter 13 (pp. 261–267), Becvar Chapter 9, Gehart
Apr 23	Postmodern (Narrative and Collaborative)	Chapter 13 (pp. 261–267), Becvar Chapter 10, Gehart

(*continued*)

EXHIBIT 13.2 Marriage and Family Therapy Theories: Mock Schedule B (*continued*)

Date	Topic	Reading*
Apr 30	Experiential (Whitaker and Internal Family System)	Chapter 8, Becvar Chapter 6 (pp. 165 and 179–227), Gehart
May 7	After-Exam Review Assignment #2 Redo Due	

*Listed readings refer to Becvar, D. S., & Becvar, R. J. (2013). *Family therapy, a systemic integration*. Boston, MA: Pearson; Gehart, D. R. (2017). *Mastering competencies in family therapy: A practical approach to theory and clinical case documentation*. Boston, MA: Cengage Learning. MFT, marriage and family therapy.

COURSE ASSIGNMENTS

The following are examples of course assignments coun-sellor educators can use when preparing to teach a vari-ety of courses in the MFCC track.

FOO Case Background and Genogram

This assignment will ask students to practice assessment skills learned in the MFT Assessment course.

1) FOO Case Background: We are all products of our families. To learn how to work with individuals and their families, it is useful to examine the family you know best: your own FOO, whether adopted or biological. Create a background review paper on your FOO and a three-generation genogram of your family

at a time when one or more family members were facing a problem or when the family was struggling at a transitional or crisis time. The final product should be no less than five pages typed and double spaced.

    a. A family background review will include an overview of your family life cycle, ethnic influences, celebrations and rituals, rules, values, stories, and philosophy of life.

    b. Explore and discuss the significance of the "Five Clues" that can be determined through your genogram: significant dates, gender beliefs and values, secrets, losses, and themes.

2) Your three-generation genogram should include intergenerational and attachment patterns.

    a. You must include all members from your grandparents down (grandparents, aunts, uncles, cousins, children, grandchildren, etc.).

    b. You will need to collect information from other family members.

    c. You must identify yourself in a special way.

    d. You must include first names and identifying years (birth, death, marriage, separation, divorce, abortion, miscarriage, etc.).

    e. You must include tracking of family dynamics (special closeness, distance, hostility, cutoffs, etc.).

    f. You must include alcohol/drug issues and physical or mental health issues.

    g. You should consider tracking things in your family that are important to only your family (i.e., education, religion, traveling, race/ethnicity if family is multicultural, etc.).

    h. You may use a computer program (Microsoft Word, Publisher, or another program) to draw your genogram. You are encouraged to hand draw it—if you hand draw it, it must be very neat. You must use rulers and other tools to make sure it looks great.

i. It must have a key.

j. You must save it as a Word, jpg, or pdf for submission.

k. If you have questions, you should ask them rather than guess.

l. This will take a while to do. You should start gathering information for it as soon as you can.

Case Conceptualization

The purpose of this assignment is to learn how to do case conceptualization from the perspective of each of the major family therapy theories using your FOO case study, family history, and dynamics. The Case Conceptualization Form (CCF) is an excellent tool for gaining case conceptualization competencies. Read Gehart's Chapter 13, Case Conceptualization, pp. 517–544, on how to fill out the CCF.

a. Complete your CCF based on your FOO case background, family history, and dynamics.

b. Download the CCF interactive form. Read Gehart's Chapter 13, Case Conceptualization, and/or watch the YouTube video instructions on filling out the form.
1. Part I: https://www.youtube.com/watch?v=h517m5QH_qE
2. Part II: https://www.youtube.com/watch?v=VyUf60jyGe0

c. Download the CCF Self-Assessment Rubric form and complete it. Check the boxes for each section that you think indicate the level of your completing each section.

   d. Turn in your CCF and the Self-Assessment
      Rubric by the due date (10% penalty for late
      papers).
   e. Examples of a completed CCF for a case study
      for each theory are found in Gehart's book,
      *Mastering Competencies in Family Therapy: A
      Practical Approach to Theories and Clinical Case
      Documentation.*

Family Assessment, Assessment Inventories Presentation, and Treatment Plan Assignment

This assignment will help students practice important
assessment skills used in MFC counseling sessions.

   1. Select cases: Students can select a family
      case from their current counseling caseload,
      or a case approved by the course instructor.
      Confidentiality applies to all practice cases.
   2. Complete the CLC Family Assessment form for
      the selected case.
   3. Administer *two assessment inventories*: Each
      student will administer two relevant assessment
      inventories with the selected case. In addition,
      students are required to share the assessment
      results with the clients (assessment subjects)
      before the end of the semester. See course
      schedule for presentation schedule. Some
      popular relational inventories include the
      PREPARE/ENRICH assessment, Myers–Briggs
      Type Indicator (MBTI), Marital Satisfaction
      Inventory, and the Dyadic Adjustment Scale.
   4. Complete a Family Treatment Plan form:
      Students will apply the family assessment
      information and the results from the assessment
      inventories to design treatment plan and
      intervention strategies for the selected case.

Relational Reflective/Clinical Paper

This assignment asks students to reflect on a period of their lives where they would have sought out marriage, family, or child counseling.

- **Reflection:** You will assess, reflect upon, and write a paper reviewing a relational experience in which you did seek or would/should have sought therapy to address. This relational experience could involve a friendship, FOO, other family members, romantic partner(s), marriage, premarriage, and so on. Issues that could be addressed include biological, psychological, social and spiritual development, sexuality, drugs/substance use, body image, and family dynamics. Address how issues of diversity affected the relational dynamic. Address how your experience shaped and influenced your life.
- **Clinical:** In the clinical section of the paper, discuss your experience from the third person, as a marriage and family therapist. Imagine that you and the individuals involved in your experience attended their first therapy session together. In the paper, conceptualize the case from a theoretical perspective. Identify and justify an assessment you would use with these individuals. Finally, develop a treatment plan with at least two treatment goals. The paper should be five to seven pages in length, not including the front page. Please submit paper to Dr. Austin via email.

14 | SCHOOL COUNSELING COURSES

INTRODUCTION

This chapter covers courses taught in the school counseling tracks of graduate counseling programs. School counselors are certified/licensed educators who aim to improve student success for all students by implementing a comprehensive school counseling program. In most cases, school counseling tracks aim to prepare highly competent professional school counselors to serve pre-K–12 students through leadership and advocacy.

School counseling programs, such as marriage, family, and child counseling programs, are all different. Even Council for Accreditation of Counseling and Related Educational Programs (CACREP)-accredited programs differ from each other significantly. For the most part, the program includes a practicum (100 clinical hours) and two internships (600 clinical hours) at local elementary, middle, and high schools. The program focuses on the American School Counselor Association (ASCA) National Model. Training throughout all of the courses emphasizes program development, implementation, and evaluation. Also in this chapter are contributions from Dr. Emily Goodman-Scott and Dr. April Megginson. They share their experiences teaching a course in this track.

COURSE DESCRIPTION

Each school counseling program offers its own unique courses, some of which are influenced by community feedback. Some of the courses offered in this track are Professional Issues in School Counseling, School Counseling Groups, School Culture, Classroom Management, Counseling Children and Adolescents in School Settings, School Counseling, and as mentioned, a school placement practicum and internship.

School counseling courses that focus on group work prepare students to facilitate groups for children in grades K–12. While this course may have some common elements related to a program's Group Counseling course, the school counseling track focuses on the roles and therapeutic factors of group work in schools. Courses that focus on the professional issues in school counseling emphasize the role of today's school counseling. Issues such as being a leader and advocate in schools and delivering school counseling programs to all students are discussed. Courses covering school culture and/or classroom management address cultural, economic, political, and legal issues in schools. Children and Adolescents in Schools courses are similar to Child and Adolescents courses in the Marriage, Family, and Child Counseling (MFCC) track; however, special attention is paid to counseling skills, theories, and techniques that can be used in schools. The key element in the Children and Adolescents course is that counseling students are trained to promote students' academic success in grades K–12. Most school counseling tracks will have a course focusing on Program Development. In this course students learn about collecting and analyzing data, conducting assessments, and implementing and evaluating a systemic school counseling program.

COURSE OBJECTIVES

Each course in this track has its own unique objectives. This section outlines some of the general objectives of these courses. Upon completion of the courses within this track, students will have several competencies. Students will be able to communicate basic history and current trends in school counseling. Students will be able to develop a comprehensive school counseling program for the K–12 school level, including individual, small group, and large group programming. Students will identify ways they can serve as agents of change within the school's culture and climate. Students will demonstrate an understanding of the cultural, economic, political, and legal issues in schools today. Students will be able to identify and understand the social, psychological, and emotional concerns of children and adolescents. Students may also learn how to respond to traumatic events in schools such as shootings and bomb threats.

MUST-COVER TOPICS

School counseling courses are often packed with information for counseling students. The role of the school counselor is constantly growing, becoming more demanding and complex. School counselor educators are doing everything to keep up with the ever-changing landscape. The following is a list of important topics discussed throughout various courses in this track. Some of these topics are briefly described.

- ASCA National Model (This is a framework school counselors can use to build school counseling programs in their schools; it can be used as a guide for school counselors so that their programming is data informed, systemic, and developmentally appropriate and improves student attendance, social and emotional health, discipline, and achievement.)
- Comprehensive school counseling program (This is designed to cover the foundations of counseling which become part of the fabric of the school's learning environment.)

- Who are school counselors (These are certified and/or licensed educators with specialized training in counseling who implement a comprehensive school counseling program aimed at improving all students' success.)
- Role of the school counselor
- Appropriate and inappropriate activities for school counselors
  - School counselors should spend a majority of their time in direct service to students. As the appropriate ratio is one school counselor for every 250 students, direct service is not always spent doing one-on-one counseling sessions. As Dr. Goodman-Scott discusses later, services are provided on a tiered system.
- Challenges of working in today's schools
- Counseling theories in schools
- Practicing counseling in schools
- Leadership
- Advocacy
- Legal and ethical issues
- Self-care
- LGBTQ youth
- Suicide
- Politics
- Bullying and cyberbullying
- Bias
- Lesson planning and classroom guidance
- Career counseling

PERSONAL EXPERIENCE

Teaching Approach

Neither of us specialize in school counseling. As counselor educators, we have, however, taught school counselors. We have learned in those classes that school counselor education involves more practical and application learning than any other track. While some of the courses require more lectures than others, these require application style learning. A common question we received when teaching school counselors was "What does this look like in a school?" Every concept covered in lecture form needs to be related back to its application inside of a school.

We have noticed that most, if not all, courses in this track can have a practical component assigned to students. The Groups courses might ask students to complete group fieldwork in a school with children and adolescents grades K–12. Students may be required to attend continuing education for a day focused on a professional issue in school counseling. Students may also be asked to observe a school counselor in a school or interview a school counselor. These practical assignments acclimate some students to better serve in schools. They also build students' networks before they enter into the profession in earnest.

Student Experience

As in other tracks, students in the school counseling track tend to experience their own anxiety regarding working in a school setting. Most students come into school counseling with no previous teaching experience. This makes going into a school today seem daunting. It is for this reason that most, if not all, of the school counseling courses encourage students to work in schools, observe, and interview school counselors. The less shell-shocked students are entering a school that better prepares them to fulfill their role. While students enter these school counseling courses with anxiety, these feelings can be an example of how important the school counseling profession is to them. We notice that most school counselors enter into the profession because of an experience they have had with a school counselor. They understand the impact a school counselor can make on a student's life. This knowledge pushes school counselors to strive for more competence.

Course Preparation

As Dr. Megginson explains later in this chapter, many of the school counseling courses' preparation is front loaded. Before classes start, online platforms need to be developed, modules created, and connections with schools and school counselors established. School counselors are busy; sharing with them that students may be contacting them to schedule observations, interviews, or clinical placements can be helpful.

Like other lecture classes, a solid week of preparation is needed. School counseling courses may take longer due to the practical nature of the courses. Organizing copies and worksheets to help students learn lesson planning, programming, career guidance, and academic advising takes time. Making sure that there is time for this preparation is essential. A challenge in preparing for these courses is the ever-changing landscape of the field, as well as knowing that there are some things we cannot prepare school counselors to face. School shootings, bomb threats, and child and adolescent depression and anxiety are facets of the profession that are being researched. Staying abreast of the current literature ever year becomes critical to course prepping.

Nuts and Bolts

There is a lot of information to be covered in this track's courses. As Dr. Goodman-Scott discusses later, sometimes not everything can be covered in one class. On class day, managing time and staying on track are challenging. Sometimes an activity will lead to further discussion, which will then slow down class but make it more mean-ingful. Part of the difficulty in teaching these courses is finding the balance between covering content and meeting the needs of students. After all, counselor educators are modeling for students what they ought to do in their own classroom programming.

We try to provide students with all of the notes, files, and PowerPoint lectures for that week's class. In doing this, we feel less guilty when students lead the discussion and content cannot get covered. Since the content is available to students online, they may feel freer to listen, take notes, ask questions, and engage in discussion because they know the material is available to them online.

Advice

The following section outlines some of our advice when teaching courses in this track. Many of our thoughts have already been discussed throughout the chapter as well as in Drs. Goodman-Scott and Megginson's contributions. Our advice for these courses includes the following:

- Make them applicable and practical. Make the connection between the classroom and the school counseling job clear.
- Build in opportunities for students to receive extra training via conferences, webinars, or guest lectures.
- Connect students to local school counselors through course assignments.
- Keep up with current research in school counselling.
- Bring current affairs related to school counseling into the classroom; have discussions about events and what they mean for students as they are entering into the profession.

VOICES FROM THE FIELD

Dr. Emily Goodman-Scott

Every fall semester I teach the school counseling course Classroom Management and School Culture, which is required for all students in our school counseling specialty. This is the newest required school counseling course, which was driven by suggestions from a local school counseling district coordinator, who provided feedback that fewer and fewer new school counselors have previous teaching experience (a trend we see across the country) and, as a result, they need to learn the culture and climate of K–12 schools as well as classroom management skills for teaching classroom lessons.

In this course I first teach about multi-tiered systems of support (MTSS) as a data-driven framework widely implemented throughout the K–12 schools in our country. I then discuss how this framework aligns with the ASCA National Model, and comprehensive school counseling programs in general, using articles I have written as well as the book *A School Counselor's Guide to MTSS*, by Routledge (I am the first editor on this book). During the first half of this semester, we cover Tier 1 supports, or prevention for all students, which can be provided at the classroom and school level, for instance. When sharing this content, we cover classroom management strategies, and the need for classroom management, as a means to engage K–12 students so they are most available for learning the content provided during the school counseling lessons. As counselors are typically trained for individual and small group counseling, there often is a need for more content on conducing large group, psychoeducational lessons, or classroom lessons. During this course students also design a lesson, completing a corresponding Lesson Plan template provided by the ASCA; this is a form school counselors regularly use in the schools. In addition to teaching them content on classroom management and lessons, I have started incorporating a virtual reality (VR) classroom management role-play through a program/company called Mursion. Thus, each school counseling student practices his or her classroom management strategies with a room of five VR middle school students, and it is observed by myself and a small group of classmates, who provide feedback, noting strengths and offering suggestions on the student's classroom management strategies. Every student practices through this VR platform. While the students were initially nervous about this role-play activity, it was a helpful experience in utilizing a new technology—(VR)—and also gaining practical application of our course content. At the Tier 1 level, we also talk about Bronfenbrenner's ecological theory and system's theory in general, noting the school counselor's role as a leader and advocate in school-wide systemic change and prevention. In this vein, students interview a school counselor to learn more about his or her efforts and perceptions regarding participating in school-wide efforts.

During the second half of the semester, we discuss Tiers 2 and 3 supports, or small group and individual work, as well as collaboration and consultation with key stakeholders. Here we discuss special populations that are traditionally underserved in schools, highlighting students who (a) are nondocumented, (b) identify as LGBTQIA+/queer-spectrum, (c) receive special education services, (d) are English Language learners, and (e) are gifted. In particular, students shadow a special education teacher to learn more about serving this population and complete the university Safe Space training, learning to be advocates for serving students identifying as LGBTQIA+/queer-spectrum, as well as cultivating a general climate of inclusivity for all students. Throughout this course we also discuss evidence-based practices, cultural responsivity, and the use of data across the three tiers.

As my goal is to teach the next generation of school counselors, I value my course content being based on best practices currently implemented in the school, coupled with professional recommendations. Thus, I aim for students to gain awareness and concrete tools for their future school counseling positions. This is one of my favorite courses to teach, and I use my background as a previous school counselor and special education teacher, thus bringing in my professional experiences, as well as guest lecturers from practicing school counselors and stakeholders, to provide stories and practical, concrete examples, to supplement the content from readings and class lecture/discussions. In addition to sharing my/guest lecturer experiences, I usually incorporate activities and assignments where the school counseling students are going into schools for observations and interviews, as well as attending conferences and events. For this course, in addition to shadowing a special education teacher and interviewing a school counselor regarding systemic, school-wide efforts, our guest lecturers include (a) a practicing school counselor who co-teaches content on serving youth identifying as LGBTQIA+/queer-spectrum, (b) a school counseling district coordinator who guest lectures on equity and inclusion in schools, (c) a school psychologist discussing the special education referral and assessment process in schools, and (d) a parent of youth in special education, discussing the parental perspective of parenting a child with exceptional needs, and relatedly navigating the school system. Students appreciate the opportunity to engage with a range of professionals/stakeholders currently in the schools, which shapes their perceptions and awareness of school culture K–12.

I also love teaching this course, as it fits with my research interests, and I bring my research into the course as well, including MTSS, especially prevention and school-wide systemic change, leadership, and advocacy. For instance, I have published a number of articles and a book on MTSS (my primary research interest), as well as published a recent study on school counselors' experiences with classroom management. This study originated from my inability to find research on the topic specifically for school counselors, for this course.

I have taught this course approximately six to eight times. I find I typically need to teach a course three or four times before I get in my "groove" with the content and pace. Then, at that point, since I know the material well, I keep my eyes open year-round for relevant resources, guest lecturers, and activities. Thus, while I teach this course once a year, I am constantly building material for the course, through my interaction with others at conferences, in the community, reading articles and books, and so forth. I save my course content in electronic folders, based on topics within the course. When I obtain new information on these course topics, I save it in the folder for the next time I teach the course. For example, I recently saved an article on classroom management for school counselors (that I published), and when I start preparing for the lecture on classroom management, I will review the contents on this electronic folder, including this new article, and consider how to incorporate this new article into the course (e.g., into my lecture, as required reading for students) and whether to remove outdated content on the topic from the previous year. As such, I am preparing for my teaching year-round. However, during the semester, I typically prepare for a lecture/class 2 weeks in advance. I set a specific time on my calendar each week for course prep; this is usually during my office hours on campus, which are a flexible few hours that I am in my office and available for students and other faculty. During this time, I review the lecture and reading from the previous year and make updates using content I have accrued and reflections from the previous year, as well as previous students' feedback anecdotally, and on their midsemester and final evaluations. Then, 1 week in advance of the course, I typically email or post the required reading list to students and also share my PowerPoint presentation. To share other organizational strategies, at the start of every class session, I give students an overview of upcoming due dates for the next 4 to 6 weeks and take questions. I also provide an overview of that class session so students know what to expect from our time together. Students tend to appreciate my structured style: high communication and organization. (Though I call my class meetings "lectures," very little time is spent in lectures; rather I ask students to complete reading in advance and come to class ready to engage in conversations and activities and application.)

To describe a classroom activity: I value student feedback and welcome a classroom culture where students feel safe sharing, for a culture of mutual respect, that we co-create together. As such, during the first night of class, I distribute a school counseling position description and school counseling position evaluation to all students, which I got online from a local school district. I ask students to review these two documents in small groups and then to create a list of expectations they have for themselves/grad students for this course, as future school counselors, specifically relating their expectations to the position description/evaluation (they often discuss things such as professionalism, punctuality, etc.). In addition to creating expectations for themselves, the graduate students create a list of expectations for me, as their faculty member. Then each small group shares its list of school counselor and faculty expectations with the larger class; I add this content to the syllabus, and we agree on this as a list of expectations for both the school counseling students and me. This becomes a sort of contract, so I know what they expect of me, and they hold each other accountable for their expectations for each other. Students generating expectations increase their buy-in and accountability and also relate these expectations to their futures as school counselors. I tell them that everything we learn/do in class should translate to their future school counseling roles. Similarly, another activity is that every semester I solicit anonymous midsemester student feedback via an online survey and review all feedback with the class the following week. Together we discuss strengths and challenges in the class, and I make changes to the course structure, based on themes in the feedback. In both these activities, students appreciate this collaborative approach and that their voices are heard. I find this also strengthens our rapport and their engagement in the course, when we have a classroom of mutual respect, collaboration, and care.

To stay on track during class, I have a time-keeper who gives us a 15-minute and 5-minute warning to when class is ending. I also give students the option of a 15-minute break during the middle of class or to end class 15 minutes early. During class, if students are engaged in a conversation or activity, I prioritize staying with that activity, rather than rushing to get to everything on our agenda. As a result, I may move missed content to subsequent weeks, add an online component, eliminate the content, or provide a brief alternative.

When grading papers, I estimate the time needed and block that time in my calendar, usually during office hours or evenings, depending on the level of feedback I anticipate giving. When grading I use the time-intensive "mastery" approach, meaning, students who demonstrate effort on an assignment and lose points on an assignment have the opportunity to apply my feedback and resubmit the assignment, for the option of earning points back. Though more time-consuming for me, I find this mastery approach ensures students gain knowledge and decreases their anxiety.

Just as I teach my students to use and be aware of classroom management strategies as future school counselors, as well as of varied needs, challenges, strengths, and ability levels of their future K–12 students, I strive to do the same in my class. Thus I often give a survey at the start of each semester, asking about learning needs, ability, and preferences. I also attempt to "read" the room as I get to know students, including their needs and gage the temperature or culture of the class and the interaction of students with each other. I find each class has its own personality, as a whole. Also, in this course we discuss some sensitive topics, and as such, I let students know that we each have unique worldviews and identities that we bring with us into the class. I ask for students to discuss this on the first night of class, self-disclosing as they are comfortable. I also say that each of us is in a different place in our identity development and knowledge/awareness journey, and as such, I ask that we remain respectful, curious, kind, and empathic to each other within the class, to encourage a safe and trusting environment where we can mutually learn from each other. This is something I not only bring up at the start of the semester, but we discuss throughout. I often sense students settle into this and witness increased self-disclosures as the semester progresses.

In terms of pitfalls and suggestions, two primary suggestions I have, especially for novice counselor educators: Be kind to yourself and have reasonable self-expectations. You will make mistakes, and that is okay. What is important is that you learn from them and are relatively transparent with your students about your process. This appropriate self-disclosure can role model for them that we are all learning and growing in our professional journey. Also, safeguard your time. You can always, always, always spend more time preparing for teaching and grading assignments. At the same time, you have many, many other responsibilities as a faculty member. I set a specific amount of time for course prep and grading each week, and I do not allow myself to spend more than this allocation. I tell myself that in order to be a healthy person and effective counselor educator, and also to meet the needs of this complex, dynamic position, I need to have boundaries, and I stick closely to these boundaries out of self-preservation. I also maintain flexibility with these boundaries for emergencies and unusual circumstances.

Dr. April Mack Megginson

I view learning through a constructivist lens. I believe that students are not vessels to be filled but must be given experiences and the opportunity to construct their own knowledge. I want my students to be critical thinkers. I want them to be able to identify the lens through which they see the world based on their own history and experiences and try to expand that lens by learning about and experiencing others in a different way. I think that personal growth and life-long learning go hand in hand to make us better school counselors and better people. I try to provide as many opportunities to practice the skills and the work of a school counselor within my courses. In reflecting on my courses, they all seem to contain the same foundational core elements: project-based or experiential learning, reflection on learning, and the development, or continued development, of their professional identity.

Most of my courses are taught in the hybrid format. Hybrid classes combine online learning with in-person class meetings. Typically, our class meets in-person six times during the semester and seven times online. During online weeks students will watch videos, participate in group discussions, complete quizzes, and reflect on their learning by writing a reflective journal on the assigned reading. In-person class sessions tend to be dynamic, fast-paced, and contain a number of experiential group activities. My in-person classes are 2 hours and 40 minutes long and tend to follow a pattern: We have an open discussion about the reading (approximately 30 minutes) and lecture (approximately 30–45 minutes), we will then begin working on some kind of experiential learning activity connected with the topic for the day (1 hour or more), we will process the activity (approximately 15–20 minutes), and then I will close with reminders for the next week and answer any questions or concerns that students have. It is important for me to make sure that the experiential activities are related directly to the future work that students will do as school counselors. Some of those activities include developing infographics regarding an assigned topic and presenting to the class, completing some kind of research on a given topic and presenting to the class, jigsaw activities, and so forth. I try to incorporate as many different activities as possible that require them to share their learning or their ideas as part of that focus on constructive learning and expanding their own lens.

The most important lesson that I learned in developing an online or a hybrid course is to "Keep it simple stupid." As a way to keep it simple and straightforward, I set up my course by weeks (we meet weekly) that indicate whether we meet online or in-person. Everything the student needs for that week is located in that section (readings, videos, assignments, and discussion boards). This has been a significant timesaver for me and has also become what I am known for as a professor. I cannot tell you how many times students have thanked me for how easy my site is to navigate and how they wish I would teach others to follow the same format. With that said, these courses can be a lot of upfront work to set up, but once you set up the shell, it becomes easy to copy it and make updates to it in future semesters. Do not spend time with bells and whistles, pick a different color for each course, and keep it simple stupid.

There are a number of other lessons that I have learned in the past few years as a counselor educator. (a) Students want some kind of lecture component, especially in the more difficult courses such as Assessment, Research, or Theories. They do not think that they are learning if they do not have a lecture. Now, we know that is not true, but most likely their undergraduate program has taught them that the professor has all of the knowledge to provide and as students they must gain as much of that knowledge from the professor as possible. It takes a while for them to learn that everyone in the class has knowledge from which they can learn and making connections with others by sharing their own stories can also be a powerful learning experience. (b) Papers are not always the most effective way for students to integrate and demonstrate their knowledge. Papers do seem to be the expectation, but allow yourself to be creative. In my Development course I had each student choose one of the developmental theories and create a video of his or her life through the lens of that theory. The videos were amazing. The students were able to really connect with their chosen theory because it was personal. The students raved about this project and still talk about how impactful it was years later. Do not be afraid to find a different way to assess learning; call it "innovative" in your tenure review packet and you are golden. (c) Sometimes you will think that your students will make the connection that the activities that you are doing in class can be replicated with their own K–12 students or clients. They will not. You need to be explicit and spell it out for them, especially in the beginning. At some point they may realize that every activity we have done in class can be modified and used as a school counseling core curriculum lesson, or in group, or with individuals, but say it anyways. If you are not explicit, they will never realize how brilliant your lessons really are. (d) Rubrics are my lifesavers. On the front end, it spells out to students exactly what I am looking for and how I plan to grade the paper. On the back end, it provides feedback for the student within the rubric itself, so it is less that I have to write out for each student when grading. Spend time creating a few really good rubrics, and then you can just modify them for your assignments. It totally pays off!

(e) Make sure to bring your own passion to the courses you are teaching. As a beginning professor, without any seniority, you will probably not have your pick of courses to teach. Finding a way to integrate the stuff you love into your courses will make it engaging and relevant for your students. For instance, working with LGBTQ youth in the schools is a topic that has become really important to me, and I have been able to find ways to incorporate it in some way into all of my courses. If I am energized and excited about teaching, then the students will pick up on that, and the course will run so much more smoothly.

One course that I particularly love teaching is our Ethical and Legal Issues for the School Counselor course. This course covers the complex ethical and legal issues that surround working with minors as well as working in the school setting. Some of the topics covered include cyberspace, Family Educational Rights and Privacy Act (FERPA), Individuals With Disabilities Education Act (IDEA), Americans With Disabilities Act (ADA), negligence, state laws, child abuse, informed consents in the school setting, notetaking, sexually active students, violence, self-harm, criminal activities, the juvenile justice system, sexual harassment, bullying, cyberbullying, LGBTQ youth, and sexting. Students are exposed to a variety of ethical decision-making models and have the opportunity to work through multiple case scenarios using each of the models. They also create a professional identity toolkit that requires them to begin thinking about their own identity as a school counselor, developing a wellness plan, and providing a place for them to keep important information such as the professional steps required to be licensed and obtain professional licensure, their individual and group informed consents, résumés, their preferred ethical decision-making models, and their transition plans.

I try to provide intentional and meaningful opportunities for students to learn and practice their skills within my classes. I assist students in developing their professional identities. I encourage personal growth and reflection. I infuse my own passions into the courses to keep them engaging, and somehow it makes the courses more genuine. I plan my courses and my classes so that we have fun that parallels the work of a school counselor. As a school counselor, you have to be fun, engaging, and approachable so that K–12 students seek you out. It has been my experience that the courses that I love to teach and with which I am more engaged end up having higher reviews from the students. The trick is to find a way to make each course one that you love to teach.

COURSE CONSIDERATIONS

Additional Textbooks

- *The School Counselor's Guide to Multi-Tiered Systems of Support*, by Emily Goodman-Scott, Jennifer Betters-Bubon, and Peg Donohue (2019)
- *Counseling Children and Adolescents*, by Jolie Ziomek-Daigle (2017)
- *The Transformed School Counselor* (3rd Edition), by Carolyn Stone and Carol A. Dahir (2015)
- *The ASCA National Model: A Framework for School Counseling Programs* (4th ed.), by American School Counselor Association (2019)
- *Introduction to Professional School Counseling*, by Jered B. Kolbert (Author), Rhonda L. Williams (Contributor), Leann M. Morgan (Contributor) (2016)
- *Hatching Tier Two and Three Interventions in Your Elementary School Counseling Program*, by Trish Hatch, Ashley Kruger, Nicole Pablo, and Whitney Danner Triplett (2019)
- *Motivational Interviewing for School Counselors*, by Reagan A. North (2017)

- *The Use of Data in School Counseling: Hatching Results for Students, Programs, and the Profession*, by Trish Hatch (2013)
- *School Counseling Practicum and Internship: 30 Essential Lessons*, by Helen Hamlet (2016)

Mock Schedule

The mock schedules in Exhibits 14.1 and 14.2 can be used to prepare for the Introduction to School Counseling, Professional School Counseling, and Advanced Principles in School Counseling courses.

EXHIBIT 14.1 School Counseling Course: Mock Schedule A

Class #	Class Topic
1	Introduction to Syllabus Overview of School Counseling Settings
2	Ethics and Ethical Decision-Making
3	Law: Federal, State, and Local
4	Comprehensive and Developmental Programming
5	Data-Driven Practice and Accountability
6	Lesson Planning and Classroom Management
7	Career Counseling
8	Consultation: Models and Implementation
9	State Exam
10	Multicultural Concerns
11	Advocacy
12	Counseling in Schools
13	Counseling in Schools
14	Crisis Planning and Suicide
15	Final Exam

EXHIBIT 14.2 School Counseling Course: Mock Schedule B

Class #	Class Topic
1	History of School Counseling
2	ASCA Model: Introduction, Foundation, and Ethics
3	ASCA Model: Developmental and Comprehensive School Counseling Programs
4	ASCA Model: Delivery Leadership and Advocacy
5	ASCA Model: Accountability Systems
6	Multicultural Competence
7	School Counseling Groups (Large and Small)
8	Individual School Counseling
9	Special Education
10	Consultation and Collaboration
11	Evidence-Based School Counseling
12	Academic and Postsecondary Planning
13	Complex Issues
14	Mental Health
15	Achievement Gap
16	Final Exam

ASCA, American School Counselor Association.

COURSE ASSIGNMENTS

Choose Your Own Adventure Ethical Game (Developed by Dr. April Mack Megginson)

This assignment requires students to develop a Choose Your Own Adventure game using an assigned ethical scenario and the research they have completed for their papers. The case scenario is provided for them and is informed by real situations with which current school counselors are dealing. Some of these ethical scenarios develop out of things that are discussed in my internship courses or things with which I had to deal when I was a school counselor. Students utilize technology such as Twine, Quest, Google Forms, PowerPoint, or Microsoft Forms to develop multiple endings and twists to the ethical scenario that has been assigned. Most of the students used Google Forms as I am a big fan of Google Suite, and they quickly become familiar with it in my classes. This culminates in a Choose Your Own Ethical Adventure game that is played and graded by other students in the last class in lieu of a presentation. This assignment allows students to really look at the ethical dilemma from all vantage points and think of every possible choice to be made and all of the various outcomes. Since I am trying to teach students to navigate through these scenarios with the understanding that there really are a number of different ways a situation could be handled, some are more ethically sound than others, and some are unethical and possibly illegal. Sometimes these decisions are not as black and white as my students would like them to be.

School Counseling Program Handbook

In groups of three to five members, students will develop a mock comprehensive school counseling handbook at the elementary, middle, or high school level. Students are to develop a creative and thorough professional school counseling program handbook for a made-up school. The final product should be based on the ASCA National Model for School Counseling Programs.

Developmental and Comprehensive School Counseling Program

Students will be separated into groups of three or four students based on their focus: elementary, middle, or high school. The groups will develop a developmental and comprehensive school counseling program. The program will incorporate goals, objectives, activities, and evaluations. Each group will address the following questions:

- How will I integrate the plan into the total school curriculum?
- How are students better because of the program?
- How will I communicate this plan to all partners?

The plan should also include two alternative sources of funding (e.g., grant sources, local businesses to access) for the annual plan and its components.

CHAPTER 2: ORIENTATION TO PROFESSIONAL COUNSELING COURSES

- **Why Counseling:** In this activity, students will discuss their responses to the prompts:
  - What do you tell others as to why you became a therapist?
  - What deep personal reason(s) sparked you to become a therapist (this may be a reason only you know)?
- **Setting Up Office Space:** In this activity, students will discuss the design for their future therapy rooms. Students are encouraged to keep their rooms comfortable, warm, and safe for emotionally vulnerable clients. The following factors should be considered when completing this activity:
  - Color, seating, materials, windows, lighting, privacy, furniture for different ages, positive distractions, and personalization

CHAPTER 3: ETHICS COURSES

- **Ethical Decision-Making:** In this activity, students will be presented a mock case study placing them in the role of therapist as they, in groups, are presented with an ethical dilemma and have to use Corey, Schneider Corey, and Callanan's (2011) eight-step ethical decision-making model to decide the best course of action. The ethical dilemma should reflect the ACA *Code of Ethics* (2014) covered in the daily reading. The ethical decision-making model includes the following steps:

- Identify the problem.
- Identify the potential issues involved.
- Review the relevant ethics codes and sections.
- Know the applicable laws and regulations.
- Obtain consultation.
- Consider possible and probable courses of action.
- Enumerate the consequences of various decisions.
- Decide on what appears to be the best course of action.

CHAPTER 4: COUNSELING THEORIES COURSES

- **Compare and Contrast:** In this activity, students will be split in half and presented with a clinical case study. Each half will have 10 to 15 minutes to formulate a case conceptualization from different theoretical orientations. Then each group will present its conceptualization to the group at large.

CHAPTER 5: DIVERSITY COURSES

- **Immigrant Experience:** In this activity, students will simulate the experience of entering a new culture. This activity is complex and will need personalizing to meet the needs of the students. This activity starts by separating the class into two large groups. Each group will be placed in separate rooms. While separated, each group will create communication rules for its group. For example, a group could create a rule in which only women can speak first, or members must cross their index and middle fingers when speaking aloud to the group. The groups' rules must relate to their way of communicating among one another, and they should be subtle enough for a new comer to the group to potentially miss. Once each group has its established rules, members will need to elect an enforcer and at least three explorers. Each group will send its explorers into the other group's room to try to learn that group's rules and learn how to communicate within the new group. The enforcer will kick them out when they break one of the group's rules. The explorers will be sent in one at a time for at most 5 minutes. However, they may break a rule in the first 30 seconds and be asked to leave the group before the 5 minutes are completed. They will take the information they have learned to the next explorer who will enter the group during the second round. The purpose of the activity is for the explorers to try to figure out the other group's communication rules. They report back what they have learned to the next explorer and so on. This process parallels the experience of immigrants, first-generation college students, and people of color in America.

CHAPTER 6: LIFE-SPAN DEVELOPMENT COURSES

- **Photo Activity:** In this activity, students will form pairs or triads depending upon the number of students in the class. Each pair will be assigned an Erikson psychosocial stage of development. Each pair will then have 30 to 45 minutes to take a photo that represents each side of a developmental stage. For example, a group with the stage intimacy versus isolation will take one picture representing intimacy and one picture representing isolation. Each group will send its photos to the instructor who will display them group by group. Each group will get a chance to discuss its photos.

CHAPTER 7: COUNSELING TECHNIQUES COURSES

- **Fishbowl Activity:** In this activity, students will sit in a circle in the middle of the room. In the middle of that circle are two chairs; one chair is the client's chair, and the other is for the therapist. Students will take turns sitting in each chair. Every student will get a chance to sit in either seat. Students need to be instructed to share something safe to discuss, maybe a struggle for which they would not seek therapy for. The purpose of this activity is to give students an opportunity to experience being the therapist and the client, for them to practice their listening skills, as well as to receive feedback from their peers.

CHAPTER 8: CAREER DEVELOPMENT COURSES

- **Career Match Work Environment:** This activity was developed by Dr. Angela Weingartner. Materials Needed: Large piece of paper, markers, colored pencils
  - In this activity, students complete the 10-minute self-assessment included in Shoya Zichy's (2017) *Career Match: Connecting Who You*

Are With What You'll Love to Do. Then they read the description of their colors that are a mixture of gold, green, blue, and red. Once they have read the description, they get into a group with others who have the same color combination (e.g., All the golds/greens go together, and all the blues/reds go together). The groups are then given these prompts to discuss in their small groups:

- What are your strengths?
- What is something new that you learned about yourself or found helpful?
- What did you notice about your work environment and your boss?
- Can you relate this information back to a time when you had a job that worked well or did not work so well?
- How might your own cultural background influence your color combination?

○ After they have shared in their groups of similar colors, they then partner up with someone who is from a different color combination (e.g., If I am a gold/green, I would partner up with a blue/red). In this new partnership, discuss what you each learned about your color description and how you might use your strengths together as a team.

○ Last, the partners draw their ideal work environment. What compromises need to be made? How can you fit everyone's needs (or not)?

○ Each group then shares its joint ideal work environment and explains how it created the work space. A large group discussion concludes this activity, focusing on the importance of understanding other personalities, strengths, cultural differences, and values.

- Rationale for using this activity: We often think people see the world the way that we see it, which is categorically untrue. In a work environment, there are a variety of personalities, interests, values, and cultures that need to work productively with one another. This activity challenges students to create a workspace that attempts to meet a variety of needs while also understanding that some compromises may need to occur. This meets the CACREP 2016 Standard V.B.2.c: interrelationships among and between work, family, and other life roles and factors including the role of multicultural issues in career development.

CHAPTER 9: GROUP COUNSELING COURSES

- **Groups in Action:** In this activity, the class watches clips of Gerald Corey, Marianne Corey, and Robert Haynes's Groups in Action group therapy clips and reflects upon the therapeutic process. More specifically, the students respond in small groups to the following prompts:
  - What are the group leaders doing to facilitate the group process?
  - What is the theme of the group's process in the clip?
  - How would you respond if you were the group leader in this situation?
  - What are the group leadership skills being displayed in the clip?

CHAPTER 10: RESEARCH COURSES

- **Weekly Article Review:** In this activity, students will select one research article to share in the class each week. This research article will need to match the "Research Design/Methodology" of the week as well as topics related to the class's mock case. Students are required to turn in the article 24 hours before class, but are not required to provide any written information regarding these articles. In class, students will discuss the article based on the following key points:

○ Article title/publish date
○ Appropriateness and quality of research question(s)
○ Importance of topic: how did the author layout the importance of this topic?
○ Organization of literature review: what other relevant research has been done on the research topic? (author's literature review)
○ Research design/methodology
  • Definition of the variables
  • Participants recruitment (who/where/when/how/why)
  • Data Collection (what data?/the amount of data/method of collection)
  • Data analysis procedure
○ Ethical concerns and the planned safeguards
○ Research finding (credibility, validity, reliability, presentation)
○ Suggestion for future study/implications

CHAPTER 11: DIAGNOSIS, ASSESSMENT, AND TREATMENT PLANNING COURSES

• **Case Vignette Discussion:** In this activity, students will combine all of the course content to process a mock case. The class will be presented with a case study. Then in small groups the class with address the following prompts:
  ○ What would you need to determine before making a provisional *Diagnostic and Statistical*

Manual of Mental Disorders (5th ed.; *DSM-5*; American Psychiatric Association, 2013) diagnosis?

○ As part of the intake process, what referrals or suggestions would you make?

○ Your client can see you for only four sessions because of insurance considerations. What might benefit the client most? (short-term goals)

○ What *DSM-5* diagnosis might you consider?

○ What assessments would you use with this client, and why?

○ What interventions might be beneficial for the client?

○ What might be the most appropriate sources to help you monitor the client's progress?

○ What are your treatment goals for this client?

○ What might be the most appropriate and beneficial treatment modality for the client?

○ What data would be important in tracking the client's progress?

○ During the termination phase, what recommendations might you make?

CHAPTER 12: PRACTICUM AND INTERNSHIP COURSES

- **Article Discussion:** Because a majority of the class time is spent processing cases, students do not often have time to discuss related topics. In this activity, students will make use of the discussion boards in the online learning management system. Each week students will post an article related to a client on their caseload. They will then discuss the relevance of the article to their clinical work. Each student will be responsible to comment on every peer's article. The instructor will also participate in these discussions. This activity helps to broaden the clinical discussions from supervision without taking time away from processing clinical issues.

CHAPTER 13: MARRIAGE, COUPLE, AND FAMILY COUNSELING COURSES

- **Build a System Activity:** In this activity, students will have an opportunity to construct a genogram, identify generational issues, detect feedback loops, and plan interventions. The students will complete this activity as a class. The instructor will create a genogram with family members that the class makes up. The class will also cocreate the problems experienced by the identified patient, as well as elements of the system such as structure, closeness, marriages, divorce, mental health issues, alcoholism, and other issues. Once the genogram is complete, (with relational lines drawn and a picture of the family is clear), students will volunteer to act out a scene as if they were members of the family for 10 to 15 minutes. During this time, the class is instructed to observe the structure of the family, the hierarchy, communication styles, structure, and feedback loops. This activity gives students a chance to put into practice the concepts they are learning theoretically.

CHAPTER 14: SCHOOL COUNSELING COURSES

- **Defining the Role:** The role of a school counselor is in flux as the needs of students change from school to school. However, it is important for school counselors to graduate with a firm professional identity. In this activity, students will be divided into small groups and tasked to craft a brief description of school counseling. Once the group crafts their statements, they will then write it on the whiteboard in class. After 15 to 20 minutes or all of the groups have placed their description upon the board, the whole class will use these statements to craft one collective defining description of school counseling upon which all students can agree.

REFERENCES

American Counseling Association. (2014). *ACA code of ethics*. Alexandria, VA: Author.

American Psychiatric Association. (2013). *Diagnostic and statistical manual of mental disorders* (5th ed.). Arlington, VA: American Psychiatric Publishing.

Corey, G., Schneider Corey, M., & Callanan, P. (2011). *Issues and ethics in the helping professions* (8th ed.). Belmont, CA: Brooks/Cole, Cengage Learning.

Zichy, S. (2017). *Career match: Connecting who you are with what you'll love to do*. Broadway, NY: American Management Association.

APPENDIX: COUNCIL FOR ACCREDITATION OF COUNSELING AND RELATED EDUCATIONAL PROGRAMS (CACREP) ALIGNMENT

Council for Accreditation of Counseling and Related Educational Programs (CACREP) Alignment

Course	Assignments	CACREP Standards
Professional Orientation	• Counseling experience assignment • Annotated bibliography/literature review and advocacy project • Action reflection paper assignment	• 2.F.1.b; 2.F.1.l • 2.F.1.a; 2.F.1.d; 2.F.1.e • 2.F.1.b; 2.F.1.h; 2.F.1.l
Ethics	• Article review • Ethics hearing and reflection paper • Informed consent • Ethical summary	• 2.F.1.i • 2.F.1.b; 2.F.1.d • 2.F.1.i • 2.F.1.i
Counseling Theories	• Theory comparison paper • Weekly journal • Preliminary theoretical "leanings" paper	• 2.F.5.a; 2.F.5.c; 2.F.5.g; 2.F.5.j • 2.F.5.a; 2.F.5.c; 2.F.5.f; 2.F.5.g • 2.F.5.a; 2.F.5.c; 2.F.5.n

(continued)

Council for Accreditation of Counseling and Related Educational
Programs (CACREP) Alignment (*continued*)

Course	Assignments	CACREP Standards
Diversity	• Reflective journals • Cultural movie review • Culture of origin paper • Identity analysis presentation	• 2.F.2.b; 2.F.2.e; 2.F.2.f • 2.F.2.d; 2.F.2.e; 2.F.2.h • 2.F.2.c; 2.F.2.d • 2.F.2.c; 2.F.2.e; 2.F.2.f
Life-Span Development	• Personal development paper • Case conceptualization through the lens of a developmental theory • Adult attachment interview	• 2.F.3.a; 2.F.3. c; 2.F.3.f • 2.F.3.a; 2.F.3.b; 2.F.3.f • 2.F.3.c; 2.F.3.e; 2.F.3.f
Counseling Techniques	• Taping role-plays and transcript	• 2.F.5.f,h,k,n
Career Development	• Career theory self-assessment	• 2.F.4.a,b,c,j
Group Counseling	• Group theory papers • Group facilitation • Group field experience	• 2.F.6.a; 2.F.6.c; 2.F.6.g • 2.F.6.b; 2.F.6.c; 2.F.6.d; 2.F.6.e; 2.F.6.f • 2.F.6.b; 2.F.6.c; 2.F.6.e; 2.F.6.f
Research	• Research proposal and in-class presentation • Interview a professor/researcher • Critique and analysis of articles	• 2.F.8.a; 2.F.8.b; 2.F.8.d; 2.F.8.f; 2.F.8.h; 2.F.8.i • 2.F.8.a; 2.F.8.e; 2.F.8.j • 2.F.8.a; 2.F.8.b; 2.F.8.g; 2.F.8.j

(*continued*)

Council for Accreditation of Counseling and Related Educational Programs (CACREP) Alignment (*continued*)

Course	Assignments	CACREP Standards
Diagnosis, Assessment, and Treatment Planning	• Diagnostic vignette • Assessment battery report	• 5.C.2.d • 2.F.7.b; 2.F.7.c; 2.F.7.d; 2.F.7.e; 2.F.7.i; 2.F.7.l
Practicum and Internship	• Video session review • Master's counseling sessions • Weekly article review • Clinical portfolio	• 2.F.5.b; 2.F.5.c • 2.F.5.a; 2.F.5.c • 2.F.5.d • 2.F.5.n
Marriage, Couple, and Family Counseling	• Family of origin (FOO) case background and genogram • Case conceptualization • Family assessment, assessment inventories presentation, and treatment plan assignment	• 5.F.1.b; 5.F.2.a; 5.F.2.b; 5.F.2.e; 5.F.2.f; 5.F.3.c • 5.F.1.b; 5.F.1.e; 5.F.3.d • 5.F.1.f; 5.F.2.c; 5.F.2.d; 5.F.2.k; 5.F.2.p; 5.F.3.a, 5.F.3.c
School Counseling	• Choose Your Own Adventure Ethical game • School counseling program handbook • Developmental and comprehensive school counseling program	• 5.G.1.b,d; 5.G.2.a,j; 5.G.3.d,n; • 5.G.1.b,c,d,e; 5.G.2.a,e,f,h,j,m,n; 5.G.3.a,b,c • 5.G.1.b,c,d,e; 5.G.2.f,g,k,m,n; 5.G.3.a,b,c

INDEX